RIDING THE WAVES

OF THE

STOCK MARKET

Applications of Environmental Astronomical Cycles
to Market Prediction and Portfolio Management

Sergio E. Serrano, Ph. D.

HydroScience Inc. Simpsonville, South Carolina

RIDING THE WAVES OF THE STOCK MARKET.
Applications of Environmental Astronomical Cycles
to Market Prediction and Portfolio Management
By Sergio E. Serrano, Ph.D.

Published by:

HydroScience Inc.
329 Montalcino Way
Simpsonville, SC 29681
U.S.A.
Email: hydroscience70@gmail.com
SAN 299-3074

Library of Congress Cataloging-in-Publication Data

Names: Serrano, Sergio E., author.
Title: Riding the waves of the stock market : applications of environmental astronomical cycles to market prediction and portfolio management / Sergio E. Serrano, Ph. D.
Description: Ambler, Pennsylvania : HydroScience Inc., [2018] | Includes bibliographical references and index.
Identifiers: LCCN 2017054675 | ISBN 9780988865235 (hardcover : alk. paper)
Subjects: LCSH: Astrology and speculation. | Astronomy. | Speculation. | Technical analysis (Investment analysis)
Classification: LCC BF1729.S6 S47 2018 | DDC 133.5/8332642--dc23
LC record available at https://lccn.loc.gov/2017054675

ISBN 978-0-9888652-3-5

I dedicate this book to my daughter, Sandra Beatriz, who has faced adversity with courage, determination, persistence, and undiminished grace, while radiating love and the joy of living. In many ways, she has been my teacher, always helping me become a better person. Forever, I love you.

Ride the Cosmic Waves of the financial markets, like the agile surfer in the ocean. During low tides, she gathers strength, collects positions, and patiently waits for the right time. When the tide is right, she releases her strength and swiftly travels ashore to success, while others choose to fight the storm, capsize, and suffer losses. Afterwards, she returns to deep waters, wisely observes the Natural Cycles, and quietly prepares for the next wave that comes her way.

Langid

CONTENTS

ACKNOWLEDGMENTS

I am deeply indebted to Dr. Sobeida Salomon for providing invaluable advice on all aspects of the book manuscript, and to Sandra Serrano for insightful suggestions about the book contents, title, and description. The National Aeronautics and Space Administration (NASA), via the Horizon System of Solar System Dynamics, provided astronomical position data to verify my calculations, and the dates of planetary equinoxes. NASA also provided images of Jupiter and Saturn used in the cover. Historical data of the DJIA was kindly provided by Macrotrends, LLC. Information on historical events over the past century in the United States was kindly provided by the America's Best History and the Wikipedia sites.

One good thing, if it is brief, it is twice as good. Even a bad thing, if it is short, it is not as bad.

Baltasar Gracián y Morales (1601-1658).

1 THE STOCK MARKET ENVIRONMENT

Astronomy and the Stock Market: Two Hobbies Created a Book

This book reports the results of an extensive quantitative research about the existence of certain astronomical cycles and their relationship to American stock market indices. Using mathematical modeling and computer simulation, I studied about 120 years of market data and attempted a correlation –sometimes a statistical correlation– with periodic fluctuations in astronomical positions and astronomical events in the solar system. The results were summarized in a series of comparative graphics, and analyzed for patterns of persistence and periodicity. Using a simple introduction to the basics of investing, the results were applied to stock market prediction and portfolio management for long-term investors.

In Chapter 1, I present an introduction on the nature of this book and a simple discussion on the variables that may affect stock market indices. I reinforce the idea that the market may present excellent opportunities to accomplish long-term financial objectives with the observance of certain natural cycles.

Chapter 2 offers a preliminary introduction to the astronomical environment relevant to the present study: positional astronomy, astronomical coordinates, and a description of the methodology employed. A basic understanding of relevant environmental astronomy helps understand the results.

Chapter 3, is the main core of the book. It is a presentation on the relationship between some astronomical variables and the stock market. With a series of comparative graphics, it illustrates the correlation between some astronomical events, such as planetary equinoxes and planetary distances, and the stock market. Starting with the present market conditions, I illustrate the remarkable coincidence of the evolution of planetary angular distances and the value of the Dow Jones Industrial Average (DJIA). Then, I take the reader on a journey back in time to gradually explore the historical events in the market, showing how astronomical variables often concur with the evolution of the DJIA. I explain the slow rise and the fast declines in the DJIA, and attempt to relate them to astronomical events in the solar system. I also remind the reader about other political, social, and economical events that occurred simultaneously, while emphasizing that the market responds to a multitude of complex variables, not just astronomical. Whether or not these events also respond to astronomical conditions is left as an open question for future research. In the end, I cover about 120 years of market data.

Chapter 4 is an application of astronomical cycles, particularly the Jupiter-Saturn cycle, to market projections and portfolio management. To make the book self contained, I present a simple introduction to investment in the stock market. This is intended to individuals with no experience in investing. I give some suggestions on how to use the cycles and other astronomical events to schedule a portfolio rebalance. For those willing to accept additional risks, I make some suggestions on how to plan and execute strategic buying or selling of assets, while taking advantage of regular market cycles and the occasional turbulence. I also provide some ideas on how to overcome the main obstacles to successful investing, particularly our own greed, fears, and sometimes panic during market volatility.

I do not assume the reader has a background in astronomy, mathematics or computer programming. Those with an interest in details or those who wish to advance the state of the art in this field will find an introduction to the mathematics of positional astronomy in Appendix A. However, this is not necessary to understand the results of the present study.

This is not another book on investing in the stock market, or about the empirical principles of choosing, buying, and selling stocks or other funds. There are excellent books on the subject, many of them referenced in the bibliography. To make the book self contained, I present a simple introduction about the basics of portfolio design and management, intended for those readers who have not yet invested in the market, or to young professionals who are starting in their careers and their investment journey. Thus, the reader is not assumed to have a background in investing.

This book presents a new application of astronomy to the analysis of economic indices. This is *not* a book about astrology. There is a fundamental difference between **astronomy** (an exact science) and **astrology** (a pseudoscience). *Astronomy*, is a natural science that studies celestial objects and phenomena. It applies mathematics, physics, and chemistry, in an effort to explain the origin of those objects, their characteristics, and their evolution. It should not be confused with *astrology*, which is a divinatory art that attempts to predict terrestrial events and human affairs from the relative positions of the Moon and the planets as they move through the signs of the zodiac. While this is not a book about astrology, I use some beliefs of astrology as a motivation to test them quantitatively, scientifically. For example, I use the astrological postulate of planetary aspects to explore and test their relationship to market indexes.

This is not a book *about* astronomy either. It is not a book about astronomical observations nor is it intended to amateur astronomers. There are excellent published treatises on the subject. However, the fundamental methodology in this research applies the principles of positional astronomy, particularly classical mechanics of the solar system, coordinate systems, and spherical trigonometry. These equations are used to calculate positions of planets to correlate them with market indices. The reader is not assumed to have a background in astronomy, mathematics, or computer programming. To make the book self contained, I include Chapter 2 on the basic principles of astronomical positions as they relate to the present research. This introduction is elementary and useful for the full appreciation of the results. Those readers with a mathematical or engineering background who wish to understand the theory behind the results, or to further the research in this fascinating field, will find Appendix A useful.

I am not a financial planner or an investment professional. My experience in the stock market comes from investing in it for more than thirty years. I learned the basics from several books, but mostly by trying it: buying assets; selling them; picking stocks in various industries; learning how to financially judge a company; how to read a balance sheet and a report on profits and losses; learning to be critical of bad investment reports and poor "expert" advice; guessing the appropriate time to buy and to sell (i.e., "dreaming" about beating the market); collecting profits from a sale and reinvesting them; and yes, sometimes losing money, adjusting, and learning from the bad experience. It is the experience of someone who walked the path.

I started with one thousand dollars from my savings, with the intention of accumulating enough funds for certain goals and for an eventual retirement. The funding of investing activities came from employer-sponsored individual retirement accounts and from after-tax online accounts from savings. Therefore, I am an average long-term investor who starts from almost nothing and ends years later by accomplishing some worthy goals. I do not promise you will get rich quick by applying the principles outlined in this book. Any book that makes such promise is absolutely misleading, and it may in fact place the investor on a fast track to ruin. On the contrary, I firmly believe that if anyone applies some basic principles *over a long term*, with consistency, persistency, and discipline, while avoiding the pitfalls –notably our own greed and fear–, can achieve his/her financial goals. Thus, if I offer some financial advice here, it is a conservative one, tried and trusted by many in the past. However, any investment comes with risks; anything worth achieving in life implies taking risks. By taking risks, we may achieve our desires. Even if we lose, the process of risk taking provides a valuable learning experience during the next trial, for success or failure is always temporary.

I am not a professional astronomer. I have been an amateur astronomer, on and off, since my adolescence, always fascinated by the stars and other celestial objects, and always wondered about their mysteries and their effects on the Earth. During my years as an individual investor, I noticed certain coincidences between some celestial events and the price of stocks. Why is it that when Jupiter is in angular proximity to Saturn the market seems to go up? Why is it that when Saturn is in opposition to Venus, the market seems to go down? Then, I read the chronicles about the disastrous effects of planetary equinoxes on terrestrial phenomena. For years, I informally took note of their occurrence in relation to sudden market drops. Is astrology right, or are they just coincidences? I developed a familiarity and confidence in these concurrences, and took them into account at the times of making my buying and selling moves. However, they were just that, beliefs. To become a scientific fact, a belief must be proven.

Why is it that astronomers do not seem the least interest in the topic? Perhaps they do not want to be confused with astrologers, a field with less reputation than the science of astronomy. My colleagues in the department of physics and astronomy at the university were frank in stating that planetary equinoxes are of no interest to astronomers. They showed a bit more interest when I approached them about the effects of sunspots and equinoxes on the Earth's climate, particularly on hydrologic series, but most of them were deep into black holes and antimatter. Thus, I found I would be alone in this research.

For many years, I thought about conducting the research that would attempt to explore and recognize the relationship between astronomical positions and the stock market. I am an environmental engineer by profession, and a scientist and a university professor by occupation. Besides teaching and university service, my research focuses on mathematical modeling of environmental processes. Astronomy and investing in the market were more like my hobbies, not the kind of endeavors you apply for a research grant to the National Science Foundation. I needed a break from regular duties to conduct this research. Finally, in 2017 I took a leave from the university to do it. This book is the result of it.

Money, the Means to Accomplish Objectives

I come from a family with a long tradition in business. For generations, many of its members devoted their lives to industrial production, corporate development, real estate investment, commodity trading, and retail distribution and exchange. I was the "black sheep" of the family when I announced to everyone that I intended to pursue a career in science, and it took them a long time to recognize I could live a comfortable life as a scientist and an engineer. To everyone in my immediate and extensive family, money is the purpose of life. To amass a fortune is the ultimate accomplishment. They believe that happiness comes with a lot of money, that anything can be acquired with money, and that everything can be resolved with money. This archaic model of life resonates with many people still today.

I always disagreed with this philosophy of life. Heated arguments with my siblings counteracted this model with a humanistic conception of life. I believe we are here in this world to accomplish something, and perhaps the purpose of life is to find such a goal and pursue it. Happiness does not necessarily come with a lot of money. In fact, too much of it can actually create unhappiness. Some of my uncles ruined their peace of mind and their emotional life as a result of their success in business. Too much money became a curse. They were constantly preoccupied with business transactions, making their money grow, protecting it, constantly afraid of losing it. In their sleepless nights they were constantly afraid and distrustful of their business partners. They were always in bad mood and over time they developed chronic diseases. They never took a fully detached vacation, and some of them were never able to retire; not a happy life by any means.

Happiness is an inner state of mind. It usually does not require a lot of money. I do not need to go to a five-star restaurant in order to enjoy a meal. I can be just as happy, if not more, by lovingly preparing a meal for my family at home, privately talking with my beautiful wife, while slowly sipping a glass of wine. I do not need a yacht to enjoy aquatic life or aquatic sports. I could be just as happy with my small canoe slowly floating on a quiet lake, while admiring the surrounding forest and fauna. Nevertheless, a simple enjoyment of anything still needs resources, however modest. Thus, money is *the means* to accomplish the enjoyment of whatever goal one desires. It is *confusing the means with the end* that gets us in trouble. Thus, the ancient question: Is money working for you, or are you working for your money? This sets the boundaries between money that helps your objectives and your enjoyment, and money that enslaves you. Accumulating money for its own sake is like compiling energy just to have it in reserve. Money is like energy to be used to generate some work.

My point is that we first need to decide what our goals are, *and then* to figure out what resources are needed in order to accomplish them. Once the goals are decided, we set to find the necessary financial resources. How do we make money? It is an ancient question treated in detail elsewhere.

Most of us go out in the world to make money in a way dictated by our family, or the prevailing media. I ask my students in class why they are pursuing a B.Sc. in engineering. Very few answer with the vocational call. Most of them are doing it because their parents did it or they suggested it to them. Some think it is a way to make money. Then, they go through life pursuing what others have told them to do, and not necessarily what they want to do. They join a consulting engineering company (i.e., working for others). Do you ever wonder why so many people hate their jobs? I see them early in the morning in the subway, glancing at the floor, dragging their feet to an agonizing corporate world they dislike, and to colleagues they despise, while dreaming about the weekend and about an elusive retirement in some ten or twenty years. Do not get me wrong, some people love their jobs; they are a minority. If more people pursued the occupations of their hearts, there would be more satisfied employees in the world.

If working for others is the standard way of making money, and the one that requires the most effort, then there is a second group composed of those who work for themselves. These are the individual business owners, individual entrepreneurs, freelance writers, service and technical consultants. It is an ideal state of mind for many and a beautiful application of the American Dream. I have a friend who proudly boasts "my business," when talking about his hoagie stand in Philadelphia. Regardless of how modest is your business, being your own boss, doing what you love, while being free from employees, might be an ideal state of mind. Not having the proverbial oppressive boss, the evil competition of bad colleagues, the stress of petty corporate politics, and the responsibilities of having employees, might be like an ideal career.

Then, there is the third group of people who decide to enter the third stage: having others work for them. Most of my relatives are in this category. Many times, it is an individual yearning that drives a person to build a large enterprise that employs people. Other times, it is a natural step for the children of business people, like my nephews and cousins. As indicated, this way of making money could be satisfying, productive, and useful to others. I have a great friend who owns a multinational corporation in Latin America. He offers an extraordinary service to several communities and he is kind and generous to his employees. On the other hand, sometimes people in the third stage of money making are subject to the maladies of excessive power and greed. In any case, this group is usually the most successful at making money, but as I said before, it is not without much stress.

Is there a better way to make money? Is there a way to combine the freedom of the second group –those who work for themselves–, and the money making efficiency of those who have others working for them? I think there is: investing in the stock market.

The stock market is where investors meet to trade stocks and bonds. Markets used to be physical places; they were trading floors in New York, Chicago, London, Tokyo and Frankfurt where stock prices were set in an ongoing live auction. Now, most transactions to buy and sell stocks are made electronically. You access these global electronic markets by placing an order through a broker. Stocks are units of ownership of a company. When a company offers stocks on the market, it means the company is publicly traded, and each stock represents a piece of ownership. Companies sell stocks to raise capital to grow their business. When you buy stock, you become a share holder or a partial owner of the company. A stock holder now shares the financial fate of the company; if the profits grow, you earn dividends from the profits and the share price appreciates in value; if the profits fall, you lose money. In addition, the price of a stock is determined by a resolution between buyers demand –investors' bid for the price–, and sellers supply of shares at a price.

Stocks are listed on the market by short symbolic names known as *ticker symbols*. For example, when you search the ticker symbol "STZ" on your broker's website, the full name of the company represented by the ticker symbol –Constellation Brands– is displayed along with the last price quoted. This price is the amount investors paid for the most recent lot of shares of that company. The goal of the average investor is to buy the stock of a company, hold it for a while, and then sell it at a higher price. Prices on markets move quickly, as demand for stocks changes along with the latest news and investors' sentiment. Thus, the price quoted for a stock may not be exactly the price you pay when you try to buy it.

It has been demonstrated in the past that if an average investor follows certain basic rules *over a long term*, s/he can achieve financial goals and make a profit. Please note that I am not advocating abandoning a career in order to devote one's life to investing in the stock market. I am simply saying that investing in the market can help you achieve goals *while* you pursue a worthy occupation and career. I have always advised my students to choose a career from the heart, regardless of how unprofitable it may appear. Doing something you love for a living is more satisfying than being in a profitable career that you hate, which can bring emotional pain. A life career should be an endeavor one would do even if no one pays you for it. This is of course an idealistic exaggeration, since everyone needs to choose an occupation that provides the minimum means to survive.

I chose an occupation I loved, science, even if it did not provide the wealth other occupations promised. While I did what I loved, I spent a few hours per month planning and investing in the stock market. For decades, the markets were working for me. The shares I owned from various companies made me a partial owner without the responsibility of working for those institutions. When I chose wisely and purchased stocks of a good company that kept growing, the entire enterprise, its products, its sales, its workers, its distribution system were partially working for me, *while* I was doing something entirely different.

A successful investor in the stock market does not have the worries and stress of the people who work for others (i.e., people in the first group of the money making scale). It allows the freedom to work for one self (i.e., people in the second group). In addition, it brings the benefits similar to those of people who have others working for them (i.e., people in the third group), but without their stress, responsibilities, and political intrigue.

It is estimated that over half of American workers are invested in the market, or their employer-sponsor accounts invest in the market. That makes them collectively co-owners of the companies they invest. In the 19th century, Karl Marx advocated that the employees of a company should be the collective owners of it. What would he say today, observing the transformation of the average employee into a collective owner of many companies?

To Sell or not to Sell? That is the Question

Buying stocks at a low price, holding them for some time, and then selling them at a high price is the simple process of making money in the stock market. What stocks to buy is a question that requires some research. The casual investor buys following his or her emotions; or after some tip in the media; or perhaps a friend has made a lot of money with a stock and urges you to buy it; or a financial planner makes that decision for you, sometimes motivated by a high commission; or there is a hysterical belief that this industry is going to explode with great profits, usually without any financial history. Then, more and more people buy the stock on impulse and indeed the share price keeps going up, until one day something triggers a massive sellout and the price plunges with many losses to the investor. Many people, unfortunately, act this way and it is usually a recipe for disaster.

On the other hand, the conscientious investor investigates the company or companies s/he is contemplating to buy; studies its balance sheets; checks the evolution of gross revenue and net profits over the past ten years; sees the long-term debt and the shareholders' equity; calculates the *market capitalization* (i.e., the number of shares times the share price), and compares it with that of companies in the same industry; reads the analyst reports and various opinions; reads the management ideas about new products, new ventures, new market shares. All of this information is easily available from your online broker. This financial research results in a selection of companies with good financials and good business outlook. Investing in them makes sense.

However, the price of a stock is not always determined by the financials of a company. Sometimes, company stocks with good financials lose value for a time. Investors do not seem to care about it. As I said before, sometimes companies with poor financials –or no prior financial history– go up in price as a result of pure speculation. This is so because the price of the stock is determined, not only by the financials, but more importantly by investors' mood. That is why the wise investor checks the historical time evolution of the price of a stock and observes any patterns, if any –continuous growth, seasonal periodic declines, etc.

Buying stocks of companies with good financials make sense. Traditional economic theory assumes that investors, or consumers for that matter, make intelligent decisions when buying. However, the new science of behavioral economics presents a completely different scenario: that investors buy on impulse, out of illogical and emotional reactions. Then, the price of a stock is affected by individual and mass psychology. Thus, the laws of supply and demand take over and determine the price of a stock. When the majority of people buy it, it goes up in price; when people sell it, it goes down.

If we accept that the price of a share is determined by mass psychology, then what are the forces that determine this behavior? The answer comes from multitude points of view, from psychological theory to esoteric laws. Many reasons have been listed as determinants of investors' behavior. The news about the economy is one of them. We hear about the unemployment rates and the subsequent opinion of economic analysts, which seem to shape a sentiment, good or bad. The news reports on the gross domestic product, the trade imbalance with China, and the interest rates set by the Federal Reserve. These and the subsequent opinions create a sense, and idea, that the economic outlook is "good" or "bad," and investors seem to respond accordingly.

In addition, there is the political environment, the new policies enacted by a government, or the scandals, indictments, and investigations of covert actions. In a global economy, the economic news from overseas also affect investor's sentiment and thus the decision of the masses to buy or to sell. Lastly, wars, conflicts, military threats, and interventions create a negative atmosphere, which sometimes affect market prices. As you see, the list of reasons that affect prices in the market is long. For these reasons, there exists an established belief that the price of stocks cannot be predicted. There are simply too many variables to consider and there is not a fundamental law that has been identified as a ruling one.

Yet, predicting when the market will go up and when it will go down remains a quintessential dream for investors. The key to make money in the market is to buy when a stock is cheap and sell it when it is expensive. To characterize the market as going up or going down as a whole, market indices have been created. One of them is the Dow Jones Industrial average (DJIA). It is a price-weighted average of thirty significant stocks traded on the New York Stock Exchange (NYSE) and the NASDAQ. Another is the Standard & Poor's 500 index (S&P 500). It is composed of a set of five hundred of the largest U. S. stocks, weighted by market capitalization. The S&P 500 index is widely considered to be the best indicator of how U. S. stocks are performing on a daily basis. Another index is the NASDAQ Composite Index. It is the market capitalization-weighted index of approximately three thousand common equities listed on the NASDAQ stock exchange. These indices give an indication of how well the stock market is performing. At a given day, these indices show the overall sentiment of investors.

If market indices indicate the general investors' mood for a class of stocks, how can we predict them, so that we may plan the timing of our buying and selling? During a market rally, the DJIA goes up. Then, the investor asks: When should I sell my shares before the next decline? This is the greatest existential question of any investor: To sell or not to sell? If I wait too long and the index plunges –and it usually does it quickly–, I lost my chance and my profits. On the other hand, at times when the DJIA is going down during a recession, when will it hit bottom and begin to rise, so that I can buy stocks at the cheapest price? If I buy now and it keeps going down, I lost my chance to buy at the lowest price. The concept is simple enough, but as we accepted, the indices cannot be predicted *deterministically*.

Are there Periodic Cycles Governing the Market?

Deterministic prediction is only possible under controlled laboratory conditions, for phenomena governed by well established scientific laws. For instance, the hydraulic engineer can predict the occurrence and precise location of a hydraulic jump in a reduced-scale flume flowing with water in her lab. She can forecast other characteristics of uniform flow ahead of time, because the number of intervening variables has been limited in her controlled experiment. However, the same phenomenon in a real-life river is not as simple to predict. There are too many other intervening variables in nature that the engineer cannot foresee, such as the occurrence of rainfall, the irregular geometry of the river channel –quite different from the prismatic flume in the lab–, the heterogeneous nature of the river bed that generates frictional losses, etc. Even if river flow is governed by general physical laws, its deterministic prediction in nature, for one future event, is difficult.

Nonetheless, knowledge of a physical law, or knowledge of a persistent and periodic empirical occurrence of a phenomenon is invaluable. To return to the example of river flow, not being able to precisely predict the complete quantitative features of a flood wave does not prevent us from predicting it *approximately*. Combining knowledge of the governing laws with uncertainty (i.e., statistical) analysis helps the engineer forecast a flood wave and warn affected communities. This is how science, combined with technology, develops applications today. The predictions are not entirely precise, but they establish conditions of occurrence of a certain phenomenon, which we may use to plan accordingly. A prerequisite here is to possess knowledge of some existing cyclical or seasonal laws.

Are there periodic cycles governing the stock market? This question has been asked for a long time. The first proposers of the existence of market cycles drew their conclusions from ancient esoteric or mystical laws, which state that every manifestation in the universe is vibratory, periodic, or cyclical. Undulatory waves manifest everywhere from hydraulic transients (i.e., water waves) to the propagation of sound, radio, and cosmic waves. A wave is characterized by its *frequency* in cycles per second or by its *period* –the time interval between two successive peaks, or two lows of the wave.

However, some phenomena exhibit cycles with very low frequencies –or long periods of oscillation. For example, air temperature in the northern hemisphere of the Earth has a seasonal frequency of one cycle per year, or a period of one year, or twelve months. This deterministic cycle is perturbed by many variables, but the underlying law (i.e., the occurrence of seasons) remains immutable. There are other cycles that have even longer periods, for example the cycles that govern climate variability, which could last centuries or even millennia.

The stock market indices are not an exception to natural laws. They indeed have some governing cycles, which remain elusive to science, in part because they are affected by too many variables. If the reader wishes to become acquainted with the general principles of cycles in the Earth, in life, and in business, I suggest a thorough reading of Lewis (1994). He summarizes well the existence of various cycles and rhythms that science has yet to discover. An illuminating treatment of astronomical cycles and their effect on meteorological conditions in the Earth was published by Tice (1875). He used qualitative research to compile dozens of weather and other events on the Earth that correlated well with the occurrence of Jupiter equinoxes. He hinted a relationship between astronomical events and prices in the stock market. This view was further taken by Benner (1884), who proposed cycles in the price of commodities and agricultural products.

Many authors devoted considerable attention to the study of cycles of various aspects of economics, population, and life. Notably, Dewey and Dakin (reprinted in 2010) published extensively in the mid 20th century and are considered classics in this field. In 1950, Bradley (reprinted in

1984) was one of the first to publish a quantitative relationship between planetary aspects and prices in the stock market. In his work, Bradley mentions other authors that attempted to identify similar periodic relationships. Their illuminating works were limited by the lack of computing power at the time. Readers found it difficult to replicate their calculations using trigonometric tables and mechanical calculators. Nevertheless, some financial planners took the time to apply Bradley's work with success. From a different point of view, excellent ideas about market cycles with applications are found in the recent book by Hirsch (2012).

The Astronomical Environment and the Market

From previous research, there appears to be sufficient evidence of the existence of periodic cycles in all aspects of nature, and prices in the stock market are not an exception. My premise is that an important driving force of these cycles is the astronomical environment. This may appear as a surprise to the average reader.

When we hear about "the environment" today, we think about nature, forests, watersheds, rivers, lakes, the ocean, the atmosphere. We evoke these while confronting pollution, the effects of contamination on the health of biological populations, including human health. We have come to understand that humans are affected by the environment and, conversely, technology and human development have reached such degree that they can also affect the environment. We understand that tornados, hurricanes, tsunamis, floods, and droughts constitute environmental forces with important implications for our society. Similarly, we know that uncontrolled development, pollution of rivers, lakes and aquifers may have serious health effects on human populations living off these resources.

We rarely mention anything beyond the Earth's atmosphere when we think about the environment. Most people have the idea that celestial phenomena are not part of the terrestrial environment, that Earth's processes are independent of astronomical events. Is this really true? For example, the seasons. We expect springs, summers, falls, and winters to follow one after the other, without much thinking. Why people forget that they are caused by Earth's rotational axis tilt with respect to the plane of the ecliptic –the plane of the elliptical orbit of the Earth moving around the Sun? This is a purely astronomical event with very specific consequences to the Earth's weather, the inequality between days and nights, the exposure to solar radiation, and life on this planet.

Why does hurricane season –typhoon season in the Pacific– occurs in the weeks prior or after the Spring equinox, and the Fall Equinox? We do not think too much about it. "April showers bring May flowers . . ." recites the poem, but it is in fact an astronomical event –the Earth equinox– that triggers the changing weather, the change in the wind patterns, the changes in the rainfall patterns.

How about the sunspot season, which has a peak every eleven years or so? We notice the change in the auroras, the disruption of the Earth's communications systems, but we do not recognize it is an astronomical event that affects the solar and terrestrial magnetic fields. How about ocean tides? In some places in high latitudes the difference between the high tide and the low tide could be of about eight feet. The accepted scientific explanation is the Moon, which disrupts the Earth's gravitational field. If the Moon's gravitational field has the capacity to elevate massive amounts of water in the oceans, is it not possible it would also affect humans? It is well known that the Moon's phases control birth and disease gestation periods. Indeed, we are told we are composed of about 98 percent of water. Should the Moon not affect us in some biological and psychic ways we have yet to understand?

The field of *astrosophy* has definitive theories about the physiological effects of planets in the solar system. We are told the Moon affects blood and lymph, Mars affects human vitality, Mercury affects the communication between the cerebrospinal and autonomic systems, Jupiter rules the heart and blood pressure, Venus controls the cardiovascular system, Saturn the skeleton system, and the Sun affects cell vitality. Astrosophy goes beyond physiological activity and postulates significant psychical effects of each planet on human consciousness. While we wait for science to discover rigorous laws confirming or disproving these theories, we must remain open to the fact that the astronomical environment has a definitive relationship to human behavior, including the patterns of buying and selling of investors in the stock market.

My contribution in the following chapters is the exploration of these relationships and the possibility of applications to investing planning and portfolio management. Identifying astronomical cycles that correlate with the stock market rhythm may help us in this endeavor. I have indicated before that even the study of purely scientific phenomena yields predictions that are only approximations. This happens because even if we are applying an established scientific law, its application in nature – outside the laboratory– encounters many uncontrolled intervening variables. What the scientist looks for is an *average* behavior after filtering the uncertainty generated by the other variables. To return to the example on the seasons, knowing about the occurrence of the seasons helps in planning the global agricultural economy. Knowing that the *average* air temperature rises in the Spring helps plan the purchase of and planting of seeds, even though no one can predict the exact temperature on a given day.

In concert with this principle, we seek an average repetitive pattern in the stock indices, beyond the multitude of economic, political and historical variables that also affect the markets. For these reasons, we must look beyond the daily fluctuations in the stock market, which are subject to these unpredictable conditions. We must look for periods of oscillation of the order of months and years. These intermediate-term periods appear useful to the long-term investor. Of course, this approach of looking for intermediate-term to long-term patters goes against our normal every day thinking. For most people, the detailed short-term occurrences of things appear much more important than the larger picture. We are so imbedded in the struggles of the day, that we overlook the big picture of life. We are much more worried about the day-to-day struggles at home or at work in the office that we forget what is really important. Likewise, looking at the hourly or daily fluctuations in the market distracts us from the long-term behavior and this is usually a recipe for disaster. Reacting impulsively to sudden market highs and drops distracts us from our long-term financial objectives, and may take us on the path of ruin. In the search for long-term patterns, in this book I specifically ignore daily fluctuations in the market and focus on its monthly and yearly evolution.

In the following pages, I demonstrate the results of an extensive quantitative research based on established principles in scientific astronomy. The reader does not have to believe anything I have just stated. I only ask you to read and interpret the numbers with an open mind, explore how you can apply them to your own investment journey, and believe only that which you have tried and tested by yourself. I wished I have had this information thirty years ago, when I was starting out. If these principles help you to gradually increase your equity and net worth, and to achieve your financial and other goals, as they did for me, the purpose of this book will be achieved.

"If you want to find the secrets of the universe, think in terms of energy, frequency and vibration."

Nikola Tesla (1856 - 1943).

"The majority believes that everything hard to comprehend must be very profound. This is incorrect. What is hard to understand is what is immature, unclear, and often false. The highest wisdom is simple and passes through the brain directly into the heart."

Viktor Schauberger (1885-1958).

2 ELEMENTS OF ENVIRONMENTAL ASTRONOMY

In Chapter 1, I discussed some generalities of how the astronomical environment has important relationships with many physical, meteorological, and biological processes in the Earth. I briefly discussed the effects of the Moon phases on ocean tides, biological gestation and development, and possibly the human psyche. I remembered the effects of solar radiation on all aspects of the climate, weather, ocean circulation and life on this planet. I reviewed the effects of the inclination Earth's axis with respect to the ecliptic on the occurrence of the seasons in the northern and southern hemispheres, and hence on the timing of the plant growing and weather phenomena.

While these effects are obvious, they remind us about the importance of the astronomical environment, and about the fact that the limits of what we consider "the environment" extend well beyond the upper atmosphere of the Earth to include other bodies and other phenomena in the solar system. We understood that much of the effects of the astronomical environment on the Earth remains to be studied from a scientific perspective.

Intrigued by the importance of the astronomical environment, I noted that the effects of astronomical bodies may include other lesser known aspects of life, including human biology and human psychology. I also remarked that many of the forces that affect the buying and selling of goods and of financial assets are the result of much more than financial analysis and rational thinking. The clues of the motivation behind buying and selling should be searched in human psychology, and particularly in the unconscious and irrational aspects of humans. This is the postulate of the new science of behavioral economics. Then, I should add that the human psyche is not an isolated entity possessing individual rational consciousness, but in fact it is part of a communal entity subject to yet unknown aspects of a collective unconscious.

Hence, the urge to buy or sell is dictated less by individual motivation, and more by an intangible stimulus propagated through the masses via emotional replication. Psychological theory dictates that the collective unconscious responds to many aspects of cultural and ethnological origins from the distant past. In addition, some mystical traditions affirm that individual thinking is affected indirectly by a Universal Consciousness (e.g., Lewis, 1981). This resonates with astrological theory, which insists astronomical positions permeate human consciousness and affect motivations and decision making.

After accepting in principle some of the ideas of philosophy and astrology as a motivation for further study, I hypothesize that the price of goods and financial assets, which is affected by supply and demand, is in fact indirectly impacted by astronomical conditions. This hypothesis remains in the domain of speculation and personal belief until it is proven. Using the scientific method, an objective quantitative experiment is needed to ascertain if a given astronomical condition correlates with price indexes in the stock market. This is one of the main objectives of this book.

In this chapter, I discuss the methodology of my research. The starting point is to briefly review the basis of astronomical positions of heavenly bodies, particularly of planets in the solar system. I assume that the reader is not a professional astronomer, a scientist, not even an amateur astronomer. For these, the following introduction is elementary. The reader is part of the general public, perhaps someone who is starting out as an individual investor, and who never had a course in astronomy, except as part of some basic geography. All that is needed here is an intuitive understanding of celestial positions. The theory behind this discussion is found in standard treatises on celestial mechanics and spherical trigonometry (e.g., Smart, 1986).

In addition, those readers interested in furthering the research in this fascinating field may want to read Appendix A, which summarizes the fundamental equations. They constitute the essential component of the mathematical model I used to calculate astronomical positions of certain planets, which were subsequently compared to market indexes, such as the DJIA. I do not describe the details of the numerical algorithm or its programming, since it falls beyond the scope of this book, and they are not necessary to understand the results. For illuminating thoughts about the construction of astronomical algorithms, see Duffett-Smith (1988) and Meeus (1991). I remark that the reader does not need to understand the following sections in this chapter in order to capture the essence of the results described in Chapter 3, or the applications in Chapter 4.

Horizon Coordinates of a Planet

In order to numerically compare the astronomical position of a planet, or the relative position of two or more planets, with the magnitude of the DJIA at a given time, it is necessary to have a means to fix positions of astronomical objects in the sky. We need to have a frame of reference we call a coordinate system which assigns two numbers or coordinates to a point in the sky. For instance, to locate a point with the familiar *Cartesian coordinate* system in a two-dimensional plane, we assign an *x* horizontal coordinate and a *y* vertical coordinate. These coordinates have specified dimensions, say in meters, which permit the location of the point relative to an origin and its corresponding plotting at a scale in a graph.

Similarly, to locate a point on the surface of the Earth, we use two *spherical coordinates*. These two numbers refer to "how far round" and "how far up" the point is with respect to an origin. The former is the *longitude*, which is the angle subtended at the center of the Earth by the Greenwich meridian –or the zero meridian– and the point of interest in sexagesimal degrees. The latter is the *latitude* north, or south, with respect to the equator (or zero latitude) in degrees. In other words, the latitude is the angle subtended at the center of the Earth by the equator and the point of interest in degrees.

Now, to locate a planet in the sky at a given time, we need an appropriate coordinate system. There are many such systems, and each of them takes its name from the fundamental plane it uses as a reference. A commonly-used one is the *horizon coordinate* system. As the name implies, the plane of reference is the observers horizon. Imagine an observer on the surface of the Earth located at point O (Figure 2.1). Assuming there are not buildings or forest obstructing the view, the horizon looks like a horizontal plane limited by a circle NESW, where N is the direction of the North (the true North, not the magnetic North), E is the direction of the E, S the South, and W the West.

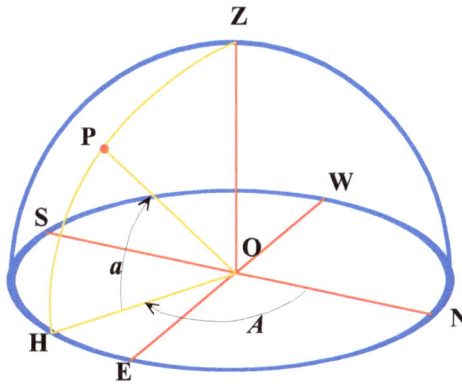

Figure 2.1: Horizon coordinates of a planet, P

To the observer looking at the sky, the stars, and the planets appear to be fixed on a hemisphere called the *celestial sphere* with O as the center. The point Z on the celestial sphere directly above the observer's head is called the *zenith*. The line OZ is the vertical direction defined by a plumb line held by the observer.

Now, the observer is looking at a planet P on the celestial sphere. Imagine a greater circle, also centered on O, going through Z and P. It meets the horizon at point H. Thus, the equatorial coordinates of P are the *azimuth*, A, and the *altitude*, a, in degrees. The azimuth is the angle subtended by the points N and H, and the altitude is the angle subtended at O by the points H and P. Thus, the azimuth measures "how far round" from the North direction planet P is, measured in degrees from a minimum of zero to a maximum of 360°. The altitude is "how far up" in degrees (negative if below the horizon) planet P is from a minimum of zero to a maximum of 180°.

The horizon coordinate system fixes the location of a planet at a given time. It is a common and intuitive system for astronomers who wish to orient their telescopes. However, these positions change constantly as the Earth rotates around its axis. We need another coordinate system which is independent of the Earth's motion.

Equatorial Coordinates of a Planet

These coordinates refer to the plane of the Earth's equator. Imagine an observer in the northern hemisphere located at point O (Figure 2.2). The plane containing the circle NESW is the observer's horizon and Z the zenith point. Imagine that Figure 2.2 is the view a long distance from the

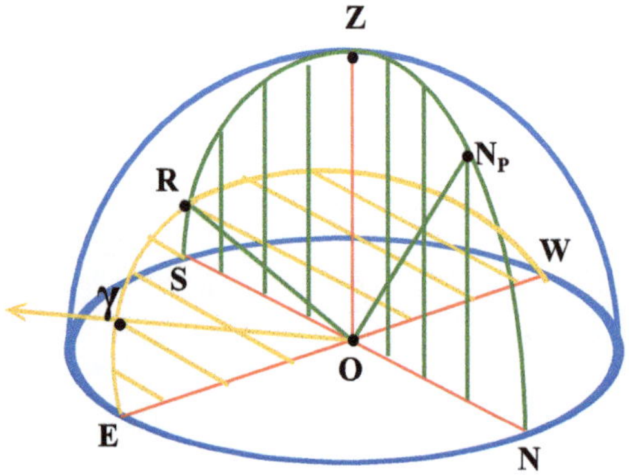

Figure 2.2: Equatorial coordinates on the celestial sphere

Earth, which has become a tiny dot at the center of the figure, but the plane of the equator has been extended to cut the celestial sphere along the circle EγRW. The equatorial plane is inclined an angle (90°-φ) degrees from the horizon plane, where φ is the observer's latitude. The axis of rotation of the Earth lies along the line ON$_P$ at right angles to the equatorial line and the line OR. The axis of rotation intersects the celestial sphere at the *north celestial pole*, N$_P$. Because of the rotation of the Earth, during the course of a night, the observer will see the stars describing circles around N$_P$.

Figure 2.3 shows the situation as seen from the ground by the observer, assumed to be in the northern hemisphere, looking up into the sky southward. The south point, S, is marked on the horizon. The yellow line represents the imaginary trace of the celestial equator CγR corresponding to the circle EγRW in Figure 2.2. The arc RS in Figure 2.3 is the great circle which goes through the points NN$_P$ZRS in Figure 2.2. The arc from the planet P to the point C on th equator in Figure 2.3 is another great circle (not shown in Figure 2.2), which goes from the pole, N$_P$, through P and to C. Thus, the angle subtended at O by the points P and C is called the *declination*, δ, of P in degrees. It defines "how far up," or how far north of the equator the planet is. The other coordinate, "how far round," is defined with respect to a fixed direction in the sky, γ, called the *vernal equinox* or the *first point of Aries*. The vernal equinox lies along the line of the intersection of the plane of the Earth's equator with that of the Earth's orbit around the Sun. All we need to know at the moment is that the direction of the vernal equinox remains fixed in the sky and that we measure the second coordinate with respect to it. The second coordinate is called the *right ascension*, α, in degrees. It is the angle subtended at O by the points γ and C.

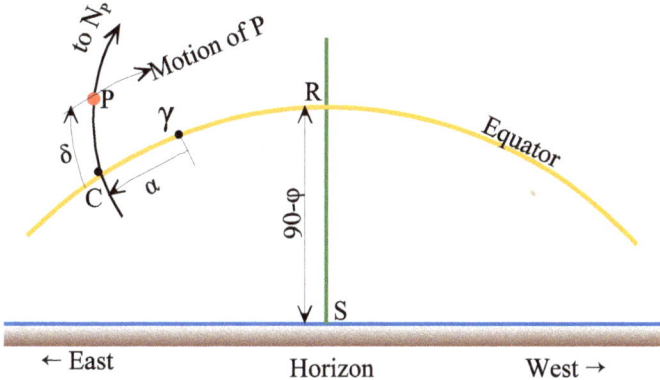

Figure 2.3: Equatorial coordinates as seen from the ground

Throughout the day and night, planet P moves westward along a circle centered at the north pole, N_P, completing a revolution in 24 hours. Since this circle is parallel to that of the equator, the declination does not change. In addition, since the location of the vernal equinox, γ, is fixed in the sky, it appears to move along the equator at the same rate as P moves along the circle. Therefore, the right ascension does not change with the rotation of the Earth either. These coordinates will change only when P moves according to its own motion. Therefore, α and δ appear to be suitable coordinates for describing the position of planets at a given time.

The declination, δ, is measured in degrees, positive north of the equator and negative south of it. The right ascension, α, is measured in degrees (0° to 360°) with respect to the vernal point, γ –which is assumed to be at zero degrees–, and increasing as we move east.

Ecliptic Coordinates of a Planet

The orbit of the Earth around the Sun defines an ellipse called the *ecliptic*. Other planets in the solar system move in orbits close to the plane of the ecliptic. It is useful to define astronomical positions of objects in the solar system with respect to the ecliptic. The *ecliptic coordinate* system also uses the vernal equinox, γ, as its reference direction.

Figure 2.4 shows the situation as seen from the ground by an observer in the northern hemisphere looking up into the sky southward. The imaginary lines of the planes of the equator and the ecliptic are drawn in the sky, and their point of intersection is at the vernal equinox, γ. The inclination between the two planes is given by ε=23° 26' and it is called the *obliquity* of the ecliptic. This angle is the Earth's tilt from the perpendicular to the plane of the ecliptic, and the origin of the seasons in the Earth. Figure 2.4 also shows a planet, P, and part of the imaginary great circle from the pole of the ecliptic, through P, down to the ecliptic at point D. In this case, the pole of the ecliptic is the point where the line drawn through the Sun perpendicular to the ecliptic meets the celestial sphere. Thus, the *ecliptic longitude*, λ, of P is defined as the angle subtended by the points γ and D. The *ecliptic latitude*, β, is the angle subtended by the points D and P.

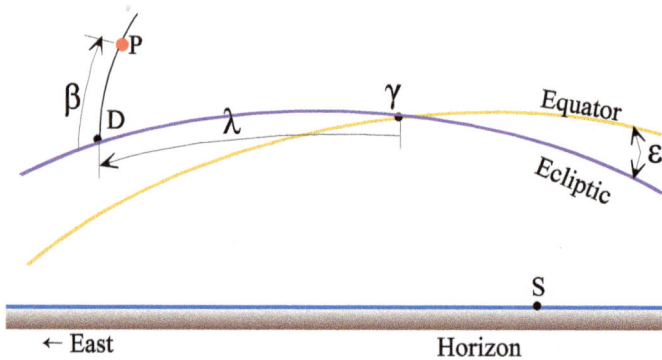

Figure 2.4: Ecliptic coordinates as seen from the ground

β —measured in degrees— is positive if P is north of the ecliptic, and negative below it. λ —measured in degrees— is positive and increases as you move eastward along the ecliptic. During the course of a year, the Sun apparently moves along the line of the ecliptic and by definition its ecliptic latitude is always zero. Around March 21st, the Sun is located at the vernal equinox, γ, and its right ascension an declination are both zero. At this time, its ecliptic longitude is also zero. After that, the Sun's ecliptic longitude gradually increases until three months later is at 90° —midsummer in the northern hemisphere. After one year, the Sun returns to its starting position after traveling 360° of ecliptic longitude, and the cycle begins again.

Time Evolution of the Astronomical Position of a Planet

Astronomical positions of planets in the solar system at a given time are obtained from the equations of motion in classical celestial mechanics. For the benefit of astronomers and those interested in traditional celestial navigation, the positions are published in *astronomical almanacs,* or so-called *ephemerides*, in equatorial, ecliptic, or other coordinates. Computer software and online almanacs are now available for easy reference. For instance, NASA's Horizons System (see bibliography) provides a useful online source of astronomical positions of objects in the solar system. The user may select a planet for desired coordinates and a date. This and many other sources available are useful for a quick and simple astronomical location of a planet.

In the present study, however, we need a means to calculate the astronomical position of a planet at specified historical times when market indexes were reported. Then, we proceed to compare astronomical positions at the same times as those of the index. The best way to observe a possible relationship is by first comparing a graph of the time evolution of the position of an object with respect to a similar graph of the market index. If a graphical analogy is noted, then we may explore a statistical relationship between the two signals over time. Thus, for the present research, I developed a mathematical model that numerically solves the mathematical equations leading to the calculation of a planet's astronomical position at a time. The calculation was repeated for all dates in the past when market index data was reported. Finally, the results were plotted in suitable coordinates with a simultaneous graph of the market index of interest.

Appendix A describes the equations used in this analysis. However, most readers would be more interested in seeing some of the results in graphical form and the corresponding discussion. As an example, the left scale of Figure 2.5 shows the evolution of Jupiter's equatorial latitude, δ, in degrees from 1960 to 1970. The right scale shows the DJIA during the same time interval.

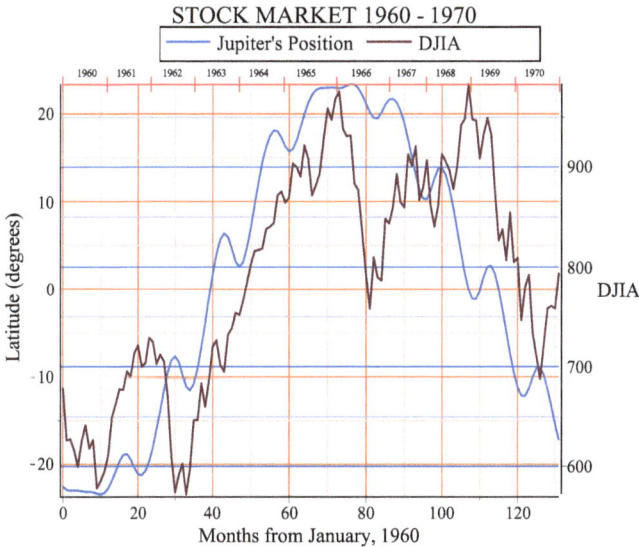

Figure 2.5: Comparison between Jupiter's latitude and the DJIA

Observing Figure 2.5, note that the two graphs have separate scales. The one on the left is Jupiter's position in degrees north or south of the celestial equator. The right scale measures the DJIA in dollars. In comparing these two completely different signals, we are seeking a correspondence in variability, possibly a statistical relation. For example, we see that in general as latitude increases, the DJIA also increases, with some localized exceptions; conversely, as latitude decreases, the DJIA also decreases, again with exceptions. This qualitative trend may be further explored by calculating a linear statistical regression between latitude and the DJIA. If we find an acceptable relationship, and if we can replicate it during other historical events, then we may conclude that there is a relationship between the two variables. This does not mean that one variable is the cause of, or directly affects, the other. It only suggests the variables linearly co-vary (i.e., they change together).

With a good relationship, one may be tempted to speculate about the possible reasons for this. For example, one may infer that as Jupiter rises above the Earth's celestial equator, it may indirectly influence human affairs in some way and affect the markets, at least in the northern hemisphere, which sounds strange. We should not be too excited about the apparent agreement between Jupiter's latitude and the DJIA. I later found it does *not* replicate well during other historical events in the market. The point is that we may attempt to explore possible relationships between astronomical positions of planets and the DJIA.

The reader may correctly assume that comparing astronomical features with an economic index is similar to "comparing apples with oranges." Let us remember that the scientific method formulates a hypothesis and then runs an experiment in an attempt to prove it. We read about science results of this fashion every day in the news. For example, we learned that education has a statistical relationship to human life expectancy. The numbers suggest that people who received a master's degree in any field tend to live longer that those who did not. One may ask, what could possibly be the relationship between education and life expectancy? *After* the results are obtained, then researchers speculate about possible reasons. One may say that education promotes a way of life that is healthier, or that educated people have more engaging interests in life, etc. The answer is that we do not know, but that does not stop us from seeking a relationship. Another question might be, does it mean that I must get a master's degree in order to live longer? I would, but the results do not support that conclusion for *one* person, only for a representative sample of a whole population. Thus, a good relationship between two different variables does not imply a cause an effect relationship; it only means that the two variables co-vary.

As another example, we read in the news that there is increasing evidence of a correlation between red meat consumption and the occurrence of heart disease. Does it mean that the consumption of red meat causes heart disease? Not necessarily. Should I become a vegetarian in order to avoid circulatory problems in the future? Not necessarily. There are too many factors ignored and the only thing the numbers suggest is that the two variables co-vary. This is a good science result in and of itself.

My point is that in science one seeks relationships between different variables measured simultaneously. These relationships may be the source of additional research which may eventually find a law. Thus, in the absence of fundamental physical laws that relate astronomical characteristics to market indexes, we resort to a comparative analysis of the two signals under identical conditions and search for a quantitative relationship.

The results reported in Chapter 3, suggest that the astronomical position of a single planet may not have a relationship with the DJIA, at least at the time scales of observation in this research. The scale of observation adopted in this study was of the order of months. This comes from the motivation to provide insight into market cycles of the order of months to years, which I believe are of interest to long-term investors. Scales of the order of days were excluded from this analysis. Short-term cycles of the order of days appear to be of interest to day traders. Thus, astronomical positions of single planets may have a transient, short-term, effect on the market. This is left for future research.

The Controllers: Angular Distance between Two Planets

My research suggests that the astronomical position of single planets seem unrelated to market indexes. On the other hand, we shall see that the astronomical position of one planet *relative to that of another* –measured by the angular distance in degrees– sometimes exhibits a good correlation with the DJIA. This is especially so for the large outer planets.

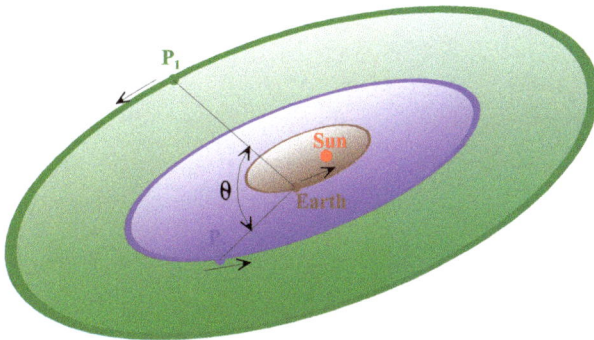

Figure 2.6: Angular distance of two planets as seen from the Earth

Each planet in the solar system has an elliptical orbit around the Sun with the Sun at the focus of the ellipse (Figure 2.6). The Earth's orbit around the Sun describes an ellipse called the ecliptic. However, other planets do not move in the same plane as that of the ecliptic, but describe orbits inclined at small angles with it. Thus, the plane of the ellipse described by the orbit of planet P_1 is inclined a few degrees from the plane of the ecliptic –the Earth's orbit. The same is true for planet P_2. At any time, θ is the angle subtended at the center of the Earth by the planets P_1 and P_2. Observed from the Earth, the angular distance, θ, evolves with time from a minimum of $0°$ when the two planets are *in conjunction*, to a maximum of 180° when the two planets are *in opposition* (Figure 2.7). Then the value of θ gradually returns to zero to start a new cycle. When the two planets are in conjunction, the observer sees them very close in the sky. When the two planets are in opposition, the observer may see one of them in the night sky while the other can not be seen because it is located on the opposite side of the celestial sphere. The time interval for two planets to complete a cycle from conjunction to conjunction –or from opposition to opposition– is called the *synodical period*.

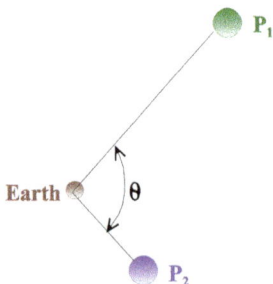

Figure 2.7: Angular distance of two planets

The conjunction of two planets is believed to reinforce the influences of the two planets in *astrological* (as opposed to astronomical) lore, whereas the opposition of planets is believed to attenuate their influence on terrestrial and human affairs.

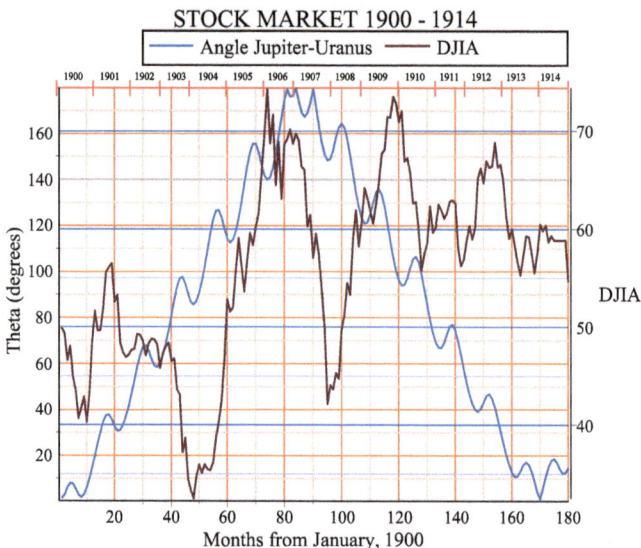

Figure 2.8: Angular distance Jupiter-Uranus in degrees

As an illustration, Figure 2.8 shows an example of the angular distance between Jupiter and Uranus in degrees for the period from 1900 to 1914. We can see a complete cycle from conjunction to conjunction with a synodical period lasting about 13.81 years. At this point, we can say that a relationship between the angular distance Jupiter-Uranus and the DJIA does not appear promising. I studied combinations of several planets and found that the most reasonable relationship is that of the Jupiter-Saturn angular distance and the DJIA, as we shall see in Chapter 3.

The Disruptions: Planetary Equinoxes

As indicated, a planet's orbit around the Sun delineates an elliptical plane, with the Sun at the focus. Some of the planets in our solar system have their axis of rotation inclined with respect to their orbital plane. This is called the *axial tilt*. This causes the *solar terminator* (the "edge" between night and day) to be inclined with respect to the axis of rotation (Figure 2.9). As a result, the northern and southern hemispheres of the planet are unequally illuminated throughout most of the planet's year.

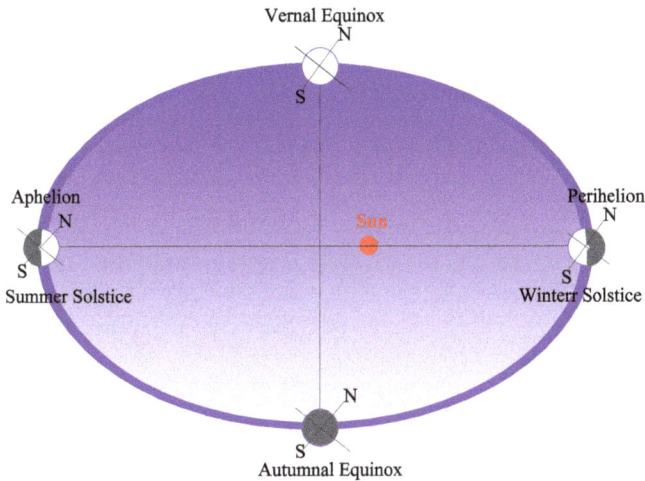

Figure 2.9: Planetary seasons

When the northern hemisphere is more illumined than the southern, then the northern hemisphere has a summer, and when the southern hemisphere is more illumined than the northern, then the northern hemisphere has a winter. There are two times during the planet's year when the solar terminator is perpendicular to the equator –parallel to the axis of rotation. At these times, the northern and southern hemispheres are equally illuminated an the length of the day and the night are equal. These are the times of the *equinoxes*. To the observer on the Earth, the Earth's equinox is the time of the year when the Sun is exactly on the celestial equator.

The axial tilt of the Earth or the obliquity of the ecliptic is 23.44°. During the Earth's year, the Spring equinox occurs around March 21 and the Autumn equinox occurs around September 21. The Earth's axis remains tilted in the same direction with reference to the background stars throughout a year (regardless of where it is in its orbit). This means that one pole (and the associated hemisphere of Earth) will be directed away from the Sun at one side of the orbit, and half an orbit later (half a year later) this pole will be directed towards the Sun. This is the cause of the seasons. Other planets experience the same phenomenon. The axial tilt of Jupiter is only 3.13° and thus the inequality between days and nights is not as accentuated. Saturn's axial tilt is 26.73°. On the other hand, Uranus's axial tilt is 82.23°, and Neptune's axial tilt is 28.32°.

It has been observed for a long time, that near the time of planetary equinoxes certain events tend to occur in the Earth. Tice (1875) compiled an extensive database of phenomena, observed over several centuries, that occurred within weeks of the date of equinoxes. In particular, he noted that many catastrophic floods, electrical storms, hurricanes, tsunamis, typhoons, tornados, and earthquakes occurred near the dates of the Earth's equinoxes or near the dates of the equinoxes of Jupiter and especially Saturn. Tice offered an electromagnetic explanation for this phenomenon. In physics, a spherical magnet rotating at a certain speed around its magnetic poles induces an electromotive force on a nearby rotating sphere. The greater the angle of inclination of their rotating planes, the greater the magnitude of the disturbance. The Sun and the planets are giant rotating spheroids with strong electromagnetic fields between their poles. They induce electromotive forces on surrounding celestial bodies. The greatest intensity of the electrical disturbance occurs when the equator of the rotating body has the greatest angle with that of others. Thus, equinoxes present an occasion when inductive electrical disturbances propagate to other celestial bodies, including the Earth. He also noted that the timing of sunspots, with the corresponding disturbance to the Earth's communications, may have a correlation with the occurrence of Jupiter's equinoxes.

These are possible explanations of a phenomena science has yet to observe, prove, or disprove. Considering the enormous mass of the giant outer planets in the solar system, the explanation seems plausible. An electromagnetic force induced by a giant rotating planet is more important, the greater its mass and the greater its rotational velocity. While the Earth's rotation (i.e., the Earth's day) lasts 23.93 hours, Jupiter's rotation lasts only 9.93 hours, and has about 397.92 times the mass of the Earth. Saturn's rotation is only 10.66 hours and has a mass 95.14 times that of the Earth.

It remains to investigate in what way, if any, the occurrence of planetary equinoxes affect economic indexes. If an electrical astronomical disturbance affects the Earth's weather and other phenomena, it is possible it also interferes with the delicate human electromagnetic field. In what way it affects, if any, remains to be investigated. For the moment, my preliminary investigation suggests that equinoxes have an important effect.

From my perspective, I attempted to note the dates of equinoxes, particularly those of the large outer planets, during my observations of historical records of the DJIA from 1900 to 2020. The dates of the equinoxes were plotted along with the calculated features of astronomical positions, and compared to historical records of the DJIA. While 120 years of market data may be representative from one point of view, it only allowed relatively few dates of planetary equinoxes. This is so because the orbital periods –the duration of the year– of the outer planets are much longer than the those of the Earth. For instance, the Jupiter year lasts 4,331 days, and Saturn's year last 10,747 days.

In any case, from my preliminary investigation, it appears that the occurrence of equinoxes of the large planets tend to disrupt the markets in the Earth. In other words, they tend to disrupt the normal cycles, interrupt highs and accelerate drops in the markets, as we shall see in Chapter 3. However, these results are preliminary and more events need to be observed to confirm these observations.

Intervening Variables: Distance to the Sun or to the Earth

We call "intervening variables" other factors that may have a secondary influence on the market. A planet's distance to the Sun changes continuously. In its elliptical orbit, a planet is closest to the Sun at a point called the *perihelion* (see Figure 2.9). After that, its distance from the Sun gradually increases to its farthest location, called the *aphelion*. After that, the distance will begin to decrease again. In the present study, I observed that a planet's increasing distance sometimes tends to be correlated with increasing market indexes –an increasing DJIA–, and a decreasing distance from the Sun sometimes tends to be correlated with a drop in the market. In other words, the farther the distance from the Sun the more its beneficial effect on the markets.

This appears to be the case with the large outer planets. Thus, when an increasing angular distance between two large planets tends to increase the DJIA, a simultaneous increasing distance of one of the large planets to the Sun sometimes seems to accentuate this effect. On the other hand, when the ruling cycle tends to lower the DJIA, a simultaneous decreasing distance of one of the large planets to the Sun sometimes seems to accelerate the drop. The keyword here is "sometimes," since I observed instances when this was not true. That is why I classify *distance* as an intervening variable, but not a deterministic one.

To a lesser extend, the distance of a large planet to the Earth appears to have the same effect as that of the distance from the same planet to the Sun. In Chapter 3, I point the occurrence of this whenever I observed it, but again I remark that this phenomenon must be further observed in future research.

When the effect of distance is observed, we may ask why this happens. The answer is that we do not know. However, nothing prevents us from inferring possible reasons. It is possible that disturbances due to the major cycles originated from the relative positions of the large planets (electrical, magnetical, gravitational, psychical, etc.) are enhanced by distance. In other words, it seems that distance accentuates whatever disturbance is in effect due to other causes. In simple terms, I would say that *getting closer to one of the greater planets is bad for the markets.*

Summary of Methodology

Having described the basic elements of the astronomical environment that appear to be correlated with economic indexes in the Earth, I now summarize the method of the present study.

The research consisted in using celestial mechanics formulae in classical astronomy and spherical trigonometry to calculate the astronomical position, the angular distance, the distance to the Sun, and the distance to the Earth of selected planets as a function of time. The computer simulations cover the period from January 1900 through January 2020, and the results were compared to the DJIA. All calculations and graphics were done via a computer program in MAPLE.

Specifically, these were the steps:

Step 1: Set the time of observation to the first business day of January 1900. From historical records, read the opening value of the DJIA.

Step 2: Calculate the astronomical positions of Venus, Mars, Jupiter, Saturn, Uranus, and Neptune for the time of observation using ecliptic coordinates.

Step 3: Repeat Step 1 and Step 2 for the first business day of each month from 1900 to 2020.

Step 4: Calculate angular distances Venus-Mars, Venus-Jupiter, Venus-Saturn, Mars-Jupiter, Jupiter-Saturn, Jupiter-Uranus for the first business day of January 1900.

Step 5: Calculate the distance in Astronomical Units (AU) of the Sun-Venus, the Sun-Mars, the Sun-Jupiter, and the Sun-Saturn for the first business day of January 1900.

Step 6: Calculate the distance in AU of the Earth-Venus, the Earth-Mars, the Earth-Jupiter, the and Earth-Saturn for the first business day of January 1900.

Step 7: Repeat Step 4 through Step 6 for the first business day of each month from 1900 to 2020.

Step 8: Plot each of the astronomical features calculated in Step 7 with a simultaneous graph of the time evolution of the DJIA from 1900 to 2020. Mark in the graphs the occurrence of equinoxes of the large planets.

Step 9: Optionally, for those astronomical features whose graphs showed a good direct relationship with the DJIA, calculate a linear statistical regression model for the periods of good agreement, with the correlation coefficient, and the 95% confidence band.

Step 10: Analysis and conclusions.

Note that I use a time step of one month, since the primary focus of the study was to identify periods of oscillation of the order of months to years of interest to intermediate-term to long-term investors. For the same reasons, I excluded Mercury; its year is so short that it generates cycles of very short duration. Similarly, short cycles that were affected by the annual evolution of the Earth were not studied in detail. On the other hand, very long cycles generated by the farthest planets, such as Neptune and Pluto (no longer considered a planet), were not studied in detail. We will have to wait until a sufficiently long record of market indexes may be compared to their astronomical features. Chapter 3 reports the most promising results.

"...We were asking ourselves: is it possible to draw in our spirit a true map of the universe, navigate according to this map towards definitive ends, and reach our chosen port? I believe our answer should be the following: human thinking cannot draw a precise map of the universe. It cannot set as goal the far and mythical shores of the kingdom of Utopia, but like the ancient navigators, it can bravely go from shipwreck to shipwreck, and from archipelago to archipelago, using the knowledge acquired by its ancestors, about the immutable constellations and about the capricious storms, completing this ancestral wisdom with actual experience, and observing the stars, the tides and the winds. This is sufficient, and the prudent Ulysses did not ask anything else from the gods."

André Maurois (1885 - 1967). "An Art of Living." SpiralPress, Ambler, PA, English translation edition by Sergio E. Serrano, 2007.

3 THE JUPITER-SATURN CYCLE

The Effect of Planetary Cycles on the Market

In previous chapters, we discussed that stock market indices, such as the DJIA, the NASDAQ, or the S&P500, respond to share prices of companies, which fluctuate according to market forces driven by investors buying and selling. These in principle depend on economic indicators, such as the prevailing prime interest rates, the economic growth, the inflation rate, the unemployment rate, and the annual rate of productivity, to name a few. Share prices of a particular company also depend on the financial report and future outlook of the company in relation to its industry and its competitors. These include the growth in annual sales, net profits, long-term debt, and assets. Investors also look at plans management has for new products, new ventures, or new markets.

In addition economic and financial indicators that cannot ignore, the national political climate and the global economic outlook have an effect on market prices. A wise investor takes into consideration these and other deterministic data before deciding on buying or selling shares in the market. However, we discussed that company financials and economic indicators have an intrinsic, but not direct, effect on share prices. Many times, good financial data about a company does not translate in investors favor and, on the contrary, its shares drop in value or remain stagnant over time. Furthermore, sometimes companies with poor financials experience a rapid growth in share prices due to investors' frenzy. This is often due to a perceived future growth of a company, based on little else but pure speculation.

For instance, a message that a given startup will be "the next Google" spreads through the media, and soon after thousands of investors jump in to buy its shares, fearing they will miss out on a great opportunity. As a result, the share price of a company that has little or nothing to offer in terms of historical gains or productivity rises dramatically. Alternatively, a reputable financial analyst publishes a report downgrading the ratings of a certain company and suggests it will be ill positioned to handle an impending change in market conditions, and soon after investors rush to sell its shares. As a result, the share price of a company with solid financials and sustained growth decreases substantially. While this is often startling to the conservative long-term investor, the fact remains that the price of a share is determined by *what investors think* of the financial, economic, political, and business environment, and not necessarily by the financial facts themselves.

This phenomenon constitutes a mass psychology, where investors replicate in group an emotional reaction to the perceived economic and political arena, and their feelings about the financial strength of a company. During periods of sudden market volatility, the actions of many investors are the result of irrational fears about a market's decline, or illogical exuberance and unwarranted optimism regarding a market's growth. Thus, we may extend the definition of a market index as follows:

The value of a market index at a given time is not only the weighted-average share price of a group of companies in a given class, but also a measure of the collective emotional response of a group of investors.

What forces influence this emotional response that translate into stock market averages, such as the DJIA? My premise is that *affective reactions driving market indices are the result of stimuli from our surrounding environment.* However, we have extended the boundaries of environmental effects beyond the earth's atmosphere to include our immediate solar system. Planetary forces may have a subtle but important effect on the human psyche, and in particular on the emotional state of investors actions on the market.

As described in Chapter 2, I conducted extensive research attempting to quantitatively measure this effect on stock market averages. In agreement with previous observations, I found that astronomical positions of some of the planets in the solar system have a noticeable effect on investors' sentiment, as measured by indicators such as the DJIA. More specifically, we found that a planet's position as observed from the Earth in the celestial sphere does not appear to have a correlation with the DJIA. However, a planet's position *relative to that of another* does seem to have a relationship. In other words, the relative position of two planets, especially the larger planets, as measured by their angular distance in degrees observed from the Earth, has a significant correlation with the DJIA.

When the two of the large planets approach each other – their angular distance decreases–, the DJIA appears to correspondingly increase. The maximum of this tendency occurs when the angular distance is near zero. We say the two planets are *in conjunction* because they appear very close to one another to the observer from the Earth. Similarly, as the two planets get further apart –their angular distance increases–, the DJIA appears to correspondingly decrease. The minimum of this tendency occurs when the angular distance is near 180°. We say the two planets are *in opposition* because they appear on opposite sides of the celestial sphere.

I described before possible explanations for this phenomenon, including those from ancient philosophy, traditional, folkloric, and astrological lore. In this chapter, I describe its observable and statistical correlation. Future research may shed some additional light on the causes. The fact remains that as the angular distance decreases, the DJIA increases, as if the effect of the two planets in question reinforces each other, their influence doubles, and this causes a positive sentiment translated into a bull market. Likewise, as the angular distance increases the DJIA decreases, as if the effects of the two planets in question cancel each other, and this causes a negative pessimistic sentiment translated into a bear market.

From above, the angular distance between two planets has an inverse relationship with the DJIA. To translate this inverse relationship into a direct one, which makes graphical analysis easier, I define the *Market*

Growth Potential (MGP) of two planets in degrees as the supplement of their angular distance. Remembering this concept from geometry, two angles are supplementary when their sum yields 180°. Hence, the MGP=180-θ, where θ is the angular distance between the two planets in degrees. We called it a "potential" growth as an analogy with similar concepts in physics, such as energy potential. The greater the energy potential, the greater its possible manifestation into physical work. Hence, the greater the MGP the greater its possible manifestation into actual market growth. However, a potential represents a possibility of manifestation and not an imminent realization. By analogy, a high value in the MGP may or may not manifest into a correspondingly high DJIA. Weather or not this occurs, depends on many other intervening variables that may affect, disrupt, or even reverse the potential.

In this chapter, we focus our attention of the effect of the large outer planets, such as Jupiter, Saturn, Uranus, and Neptune. As a result of their elliptical orbits with long periods around the Sun, the position of these planets with respect to the Earth generate cycles of intermediate duration of the order of years. These cycles, and their effect on the DJIA, may be observed. While the inner planets, Venus and Mercury and the small outer Mars exercise an influence, their cycles have short durations and manifest during periods of weeks or months. I believe the average long-term investor can plan a more stable portfolio by working with a cycle lasting years, instead of a turbulent one with a duration of days and weeks.

I also consider the effect of planetary equinoxes. As is the case in the Earth, a planet's equinox occurs when the plane of its equator passes through the center of the Sun's disk. At this time, a planet's day and night are of approximately of equal duration. Several authors in the past argued that the equinox of the large outer planets may have an influence in terrestrial weather and other phenomena. My research suggests that sometimes planetary equinoxes disrupt or even completely reverse the effect of the MGP.

As described in Chapter 2, we used celestial mechanics formulae in classical astronomy and spherical trigonometry to calculate the astronomical position, the angular distance, and the MGP of selected planets as a function of time. The computer simulations cover the period from January 1900 through January 2020 and the results were compared to the DJIA. The time resolution I used was of the order of one month. Thus, calculated MGP were compared to the DJIA on the first day of each month. I used the actual value of the DJIA at opening on the first day of each month as reported in historical data bases. In other words, no averaging or filtering was performed. Statisticians argue in favor of filtering the raw series (moving averages, inflation correction, Kalman filtering, etc.). I decided against it in this study. Those readers interested in the mathematical details of these calculations may browse Appendix A and consult the references given in the bibliography.

In this study, several planetary combinations were considered. For example, I studied the angular distance and the MGP between Venus and Mars as it evolved with time between 1900 and 2020. Several other combinations were studied, for example, Venus-Jupiter, Venus-Saturn, Jupiter-Saturn, Jupiter-Uranus, and Jupiter-Neptune. In addition, the angular distances between each of these planets and the Sun, as observed from the Earth, were also calculated.

As indicated before, many of the above combinations generate cycles with a return period of a few months only. They are the result of the Earth's annual revolution around the Sun. Other long cycles may have an important influence, such the Jupiter-Uranus and the Jupiter-Neptune cycles. They appear to have return periods of the order of several decades. However, DJIA historical data is available for about twelve decades. During this time, there were not a representative number of events that could show a significant correlation. In addition, I did not study the simultaneous effect of the relative position of three or more planets. These and other phenomena are left to future researchers.

In this chapter, we concentrate on the results of one cycle that stands out: The Jupiter-Saturn cycle. Each of these planets has a mass significantly greater than the Earth's, and faster periods of rotation. Also these planets emit more energy that they receive from the Sun. These facts may be among the reasons why they influence the Earth. The Jupiter-Saturn cycle has a period of about twenty years –19.87 years *synodic period*. In other words, the time interval between two successive peaks in its MGP is about twenty years.

How does the Jupiter-Saturn cycle relate to the DJIA? We have 120 years of market data to compare to our simulations. Let us see some illuminating examples from historical data.

The Great Bull Market 2010-2020

The last ten years have seen one of the biggest increases in the DJIA, as well as other stock market indicators. After the great recession of 2008-2009, the market has experienced large increases year after year: 11.02% in 2010, 5.53% in 2011, 7.26% in 2012, 26.50% in 2013, 7.52% in 2014. In 2015 there was a small decline of 2.23%, followed by increases of 13.42% in 2016, and 25.08% in 2017. In 2018 it declined 5.63% and in 2019 increased 19.26%. Thus, since the last recession, the DJIA has more than tripled in value. This period will be remembered as one of the longest of almost continued increase in the DJIA. We can find multiple economic and political reasons to justify this. After the great recession of 2008-2009, there was a myriad of companies with great financials at bargain share prices. It was the presidency of Barack Obama, characterized by much economic stimulus, growth, international trade, many social and economic reforms, and a period of relative peace.

Thus, one can always look back at history and justify in retrospect the "causes" behind the stock market performance. However, attempting to use the same analysis to predict its future performance is not as easy. Under the current instability of the presidency of Donald Trump, investors continue to be a powerful buying force in the market. The market is overheated, stocks are overvalued. The rational thing to do is to sell stocks now and collect profits before the next market drop. Yet, investors continue to pour money in the market. Why? Analysts point at the belief that this administration will drive the American economy to new levels due to investment in infrastructure and industrial development. Many analyst coincide in that this stated government policy –which has not yet translated into actions– is only part of the reason for the current buying frenzy. Beyond the good economic indicators, the real reasons may be more emotional than rational. Perhaps we should look at the astronomical environment for answers.

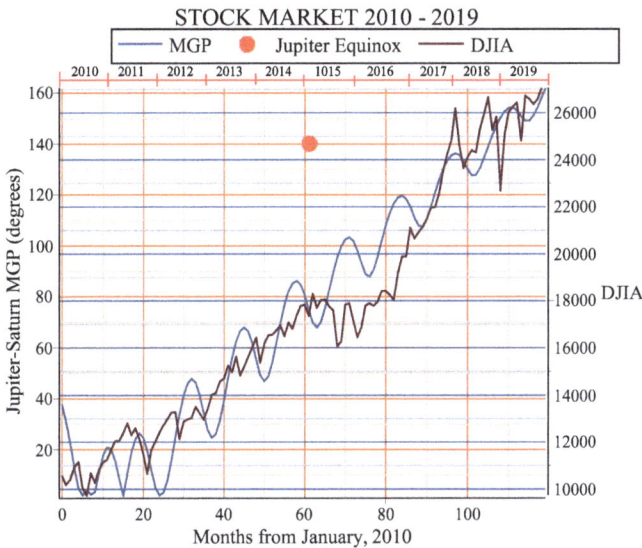

Figure 3.1: Comparison between the DJIA and the Jupiter-Saturn MGP, 2010-2019

How did the DJIA compare to the planetary potential during the same period? A picture is worth a thousand words. Figure 3.1 shows a comparison between the DJIA and the Jupiter-Saturn MGP for the same period. The blue line shows the MGP with small wavy oscillations up and down, each lasting about twelve months, due to the annual revolution of the Earth around the Sun. Beyond these, the trend in the MGP exhibits a clear and continuous increase over time from about 20 degrees in 2010 to 160 degrees by the end of 2019. The DJIA also shows the erratic short-term ups and downs typical of the market. Beyond this short-term variability, the trend in the DJIA also shows a continuous increase in its value from about 10,000 in 2010 to more than 27,000 in 2019.

It is unclear whether the small oscillations in the MGP have an effect on the short-term oscillations in the DJIA. What is clear is that the trend of the two curves coincide with a continuous increase over time. This leads us to two important observations:

1. *The MGP long-term evolution and trend are the important features representing its potential effect on the DJIA, and not necessarily the short-term oscillations.*
2. *From 1, the MGP should be observed as a whole –instead of the individual points– as a predictor of potential increase, or potential decrease, in the DJIA. The actual value of the MGP at a given time (in sexagesimal degrees) may not be a good predictor of the value of the DJIA (in dollars) at the same time.*

One should look at the MGP as a complete graph with a given tendency and not at particular points of it. By analogy, a probability density function and a spectral density function are examples of similar curves in statistics that should be observed as a whole, rather than their individual points. Even though an informal visual appreciation of Figure 3.1 suggests a strong correspondence between the MGP and the DJIA, we demonstrate this statistically.

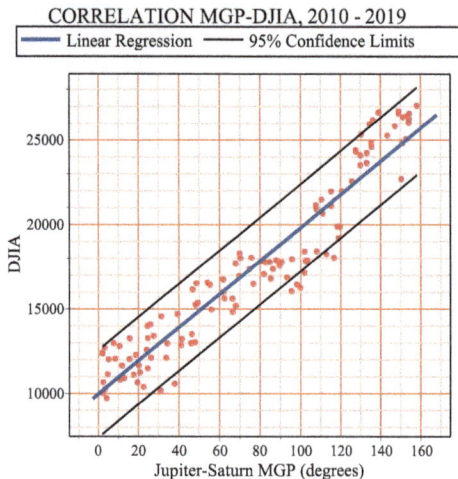

Figure 3.2: Statistical correlation between the Jupiter-Saturn MGP and the DJIA, 2010-2019

Over the time window of observation, 2010-2019, the MGP and the DJIA show a strong statistical correlation. Figure 3.2 shows the scatter graph of the historical monthly point values of the DJIA, and the corresponding fitted linear regression between the two signals. The linear regression was calculated using the Least Squares Method. The figure also illustrates the concave lines of the 95% confidence limits of the regression line. For details on the statistical analysis and interpretation, the reader is referred to any statistics book (i.e., Serrano, 2011, has many examples and programs). Figure 3.2 suggests a strong linear statistical correlation between the DJIA and the Jupiter-Saturn MGP. The correlation coefficient for this model is $r=0.95$, which means that about 95 % of the magnitude of the DJIA could be predicted by that of the MGP. This leads us to two more observations:

3. *The regression model between the DJIA and the MGP is strictly valid during the period of analysis (i.e., 2010-2019 in this case of Figure 3.2).*
4. *As with any statistical model, extrapolation beyond the historical data widens the confidence band, and reduces accuracy.*

From 3 and 4 above, one should never use this model to predict future values of the dependent variable (i.e., the DJIA), even though a strong linear relationship exists. This is a common rule in statistics, very often violated in real life. A strong linear relationship is observed for the period of analysis only, but nothing guarantees that this linear co-variability will persist beyond 2019. Let us remember that our objective here is to find upward or downward trends over time, not to predict the actual value of the DJIA. In pursuing this objective, I looked at the raw values of the DJIA, uncorrected for inflation and volume increases. Since the DJIA has increased from less than 100 in 1900 to more than 27,000 in 2019, we limit our observations to short intervals of time, which contain important changes in the stock market.

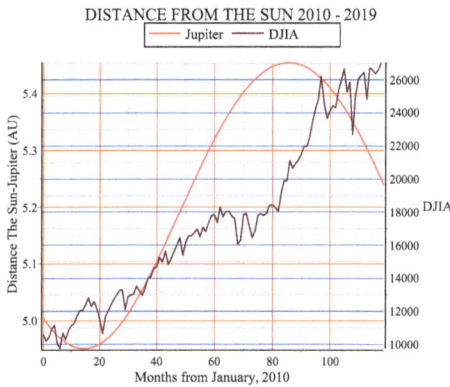

Figure 3.2: Distance The Sun-Jupiter wit time

There are too many variables ignored in a simple linear statistical model covering an interval of a few years. In fact, it is clear that the relationship between the MGP and the DJIA is *nonlinear* over long periods of time. One of the reasons why science resorts to statistics is because, when failing to identify a cause-effect relationship of a phenomenon (i.e., a physical law), the next best thing to do is to attempt to identify the existence of an empirical linear relationship. A statistical relationship, while not a cause-effect rule, is still an objective quantitative description of the relationship between the DJIA and the MGP. Let us remember once again that our objective is not to predict the actual value of the DJIA at a given time, but to forecast the likelihood of its increase or decrease over time. Thus, with the observations and limitations of 1 through 4 above, we may use the MGP as a guideline to study market potential values and long-term portfolio planning.

There is one feature in Figure 3.1 we have not discussed, namely the occurrence of a Jupiter equinox in February 2015, identified as a red circle in Figure 3.1. We have said that planetary equinoxes may have a disruptive effect on the general pattern of the MGP. In this case, the occurrence of a Jupiter equinox did not seem to significantly interrupt the overall increase in the MGP and the DJIA. Nonetheless, it is interesting to observe that the only market decline in the period 2010-2019 –2.23% decline in the DJIA– also occurred in 2015. We will discuss more about this later. For the time being, it is important to remember that the presence of planetary equinoxes, especially those from the large outer planets, may affect or even reverse the calculations. Chapter 2 included hypotheses given by other authors to explain this phenomenon.

In attempting to discern why Jupiter's equinox did not significantly alter the general pattern of the MGP and the DJIA, we offer an additional variable that our simulations suggest it may intervene: The distance between the Sun and Jupiter, and not necessarily that between the planet and the Earth. Figure 3.3 illustrates the distance in Astronomical Units (AU) between the Sun and Jupiter as it changes with time during the period 2010-2019. One Astronomical Unit equals 149.6 million kilometers. The graph shows a continuous and gradual increase in the distance between about 4.9 AU in 2010 and about 5.5 AU in 2017, followed by a gradual decline after that. Tice (1875) suggested that Jupiter exerts an energetic influence on the Sun, the magnitude of which increases as Jupiter approaches the Sun. He also implied a relation between distance and the sunspot cycle, which incidently has an average duration of about 11 years. The Jupiter period of revolution, and thus the period of its distance from the sun, is about 11.86 years. The sunspot cycle is known to be accompanied by enormous electromagnetic emissions and energy flares that disrupt the Earth's weather and communications. This is an active area of research and we do not know for sure the relationship between the sunspot cycle and Jupiter, or its effect on the stock market for that matter. For our purposes, we may speculate that an increasing distance between the Sun and Jupiter, as exemplified in Figure 3.3, may act as a mitigating factor that diminishes the disruptive effect of equinoxes.

In addition to a continuous increase in the distance between the Sun and Jupiter during 2010-2017, it is also interesting to note that a similar graph –not shown– of the distance between the Sun and Saturn during the same period shows a gradual increase from 9.5 AU in 2010 to 10.7 AU in 2017. Therefore, an increasing distance between the Sun and Jupiter, combined with an increasing distance between the Sun and Saturn, appears to enhance a rising MGP, and to ameliorate the effect of a Jupiter equinox. Now that we have described the typical relationship between the DJIA and the MGP and some of its features, let us now explore other historical events in the stock market that may provide further insight on a relationship between the astronomical environment and the markets.

The Great Recession of 2007-2009

During this time, the world experienced the biggest financial crisis since the Great Depression. The global downturn was caused by a number of factors. Motivated by profit, for the previous years banks had extended loans to unqualified buyers with bad credit records. Millions of people ended up owning a home they could not afford. Bankers then lumped these mortgages together with more secure loans, before selling them on to other banks, who sold them onto other financial institutions, and so on. The bankers then received enormous bonuses for the commission and fees they generated. This sub-prime market exploded when millions of Americans began defaulting on their payments. The outcome was a collapse with an unprecedented liquidity crisis. Some of the largest banks in the world had to be intervened by the government to prevent an even bigger financial catastrophe. Parallel to this crisis, was the unprecedented rise in consumer spending and personal debt to pay for extravagant and unnecessary items. This led to a massive rise in bankruptcies and foreclosures, triggering a worldwide recession. As a result, economic indicators, such as the unemployment rate and the DJIA declined dramatically.

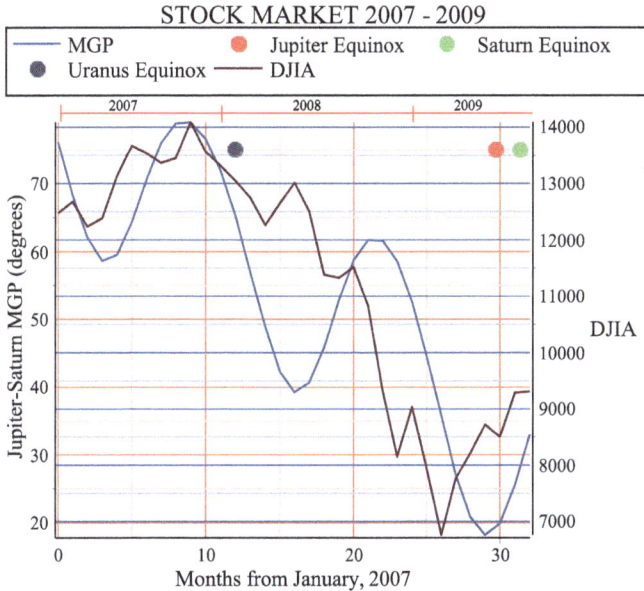

Figure 3.4: Comparison between the DJIA and the Jupiter-Saturn MGP, 2007-2009

Beyond these economic reasons for the collapse in the stock market indices, which most consider as the direct cause of the DJIA decline, we wonder if there were some corresponding phenomena in the astronomical environment, which may have encouraged this state of affairs. Figure 3.4 shows a comparison between the DJIA and the Jupiter-Saturn MGP for this period. The DJIA shows a peak of about 14,000 in November 2007, followed by a dramatic decline to a about 7,000 in February 2009, or a decline of about 50%. By year, the DJIA gained a modest 6.43% in 2007, offset by previous gains, and lost 33.84% in value in 2008, the second greatest annual decline since the Great Depression.

CORRELATION MGP-DJIA, 2007 - 2009

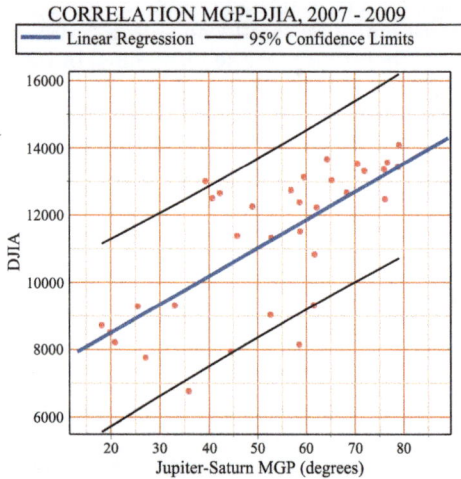

Figure 3.5: Statistical correlation between the
Jupiter-Saturn MGP and the DJIA, 2007-2009

During the same period of 2007-2009, the MGP showed the usual wavy ups and downs, but the overall trend was downward from about 75 degrees early in 2007 to about 18 degrees by the end of 2009. Both the DJIA and the MGP exhibit an average downward trend during this period.

The negative, downward, influence of the MGP was exacerbated by three other important astronomical events: A Uranus equinox in December, 2007, a Jupiter equinox in June, 2009, and a Saturn equinox in August, 2009. As indicated before, the occurrence of planetary equinoxes tend to have a disruptive negative influence, the effect of which is felt in and around the time of the equinox. Thus, we see that a downward trend of the MGP, added to the very unusual occurrence of three planetary equinoxes in this period, resulted in a highly disruptive influence to the markets.

DISTANCE FROM THE SUN 2007 - 2009

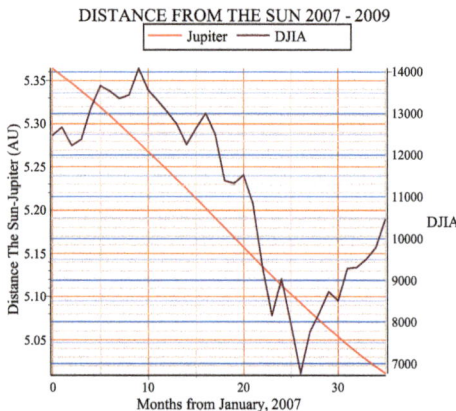

Figure 3.6: Distance the Sun-Jupiter with time

As shown in Figure 3.5, the correlation between the DJIA and the MGP for this period is not as great as that for 2010-2017, due to the disruptive influence of the planetary equinoxes. The correlation coefficient is $r=0.72$ or 72%. Thus for the interval 2007-2009 the data shows evidence of a linear correlation, but not as strong as that for the 2010-2017 period.

It is also interesting to remark that during the 2007-2009 period the distance between the Sun and Jupiter was decreasing and reaching a minimum around the end of 2009. Figure 3.6 illustrates this in detail. As suggested before, as Jupiter gets closer to the Sun, it appears to have a negative influence on Earth's phenomena, including the stock market.

We conclude this section noting that, while there were many economical reasons for the Great Recession of 2007-2009, there were also important environmental astronomical influences. This strengthens the notion that forecasting the occurrence of astronomical events may improve the economic forecasts that may affect the stock market.

The Recession of 2000-2003

During this time, online business was in its infancy. Investors believed that a "new economy" driven by the Internet defied the conventional rules of business. As a result, there was a rally to buy stocks in dot-com companies, many of them unprofitable business with unreasonable price/earnings ratios. In April of 2000, an inflation report caused the speculative bubble to burst and there were huge investment losses.

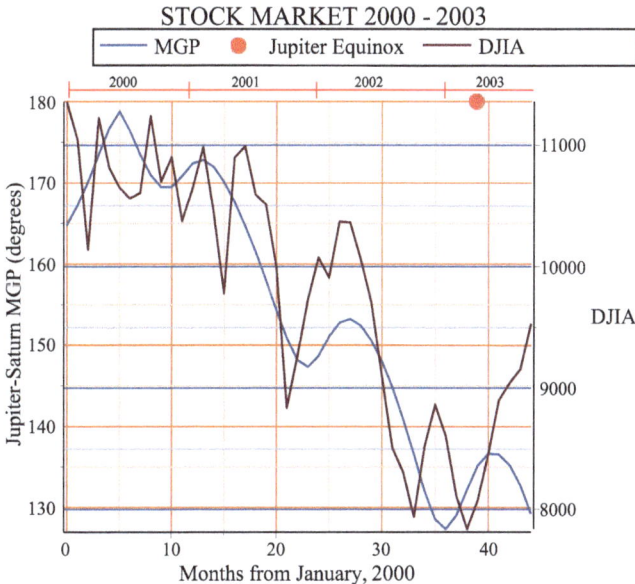

Figure 3.7: Comparison between the DJIA and the Jupiter-Saturn MGP, 2000-2003

September 2001 was the time of the terrorist attacks in the U. S. Thousands of people lost their lives and the economic losses were unmeasurable. Tens of thousands of business were either destroyed or displaced in the attacks to Manhattan. This amounted to a catastrophic financial loss in the U. S.

2001 was also the time of big corporate scandals and fraud. Giant companies were caught hiding billions of dollars in debt and bad deals, and investors lost billions. These scandals shook the securities markets and investor confidence. These events resulted in a recession. The DJIA lost 6.17% in 2000, 7.10% in 2001, and 16.76% in 2002.

During this period, the DJIA decreased from over 11,000 in 2000 to about less than 8,000 near the end of 2003. In concert with this, there was a corresponding general decline in the Jupiter-Saturn MGP (Figure 3.7) from about 178 degrees at the beginning of 2000, to about 130 degrees near the end of 2003. In addition, there was a Jupiter equinox on March 2003.

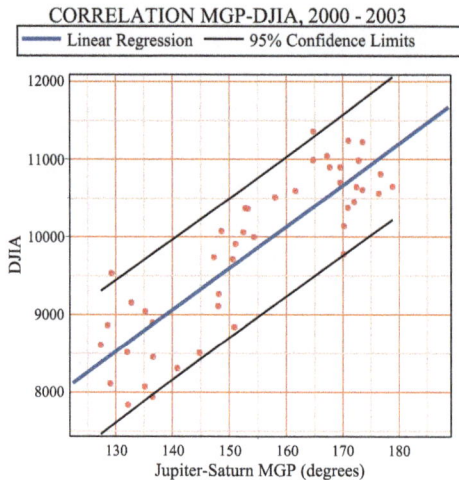

Figure 3.8: Statistical correlation between the Jupiter-Saturn MGP and the DJIA, 2000-2003

One again, we see a correspondence between the market indicators and the astronomical environment. There was a significant statistical correlation between the MGP and the DJIA during this time (Figure 3.8). The calculated correlation coefficient is $r=0.86$ or 86%.

The Bear Market of 1990-1999

This period saw a number of economic and political events that resulted in unprecedented gains in the stock market. In 1990, the Soviet Union collapsed, the Berlin Wall came down, and Germany was reunited.

In January 1994, the North American Free Trade Agreement (NAFTA) went into effect, creating a free trade zone between Canada, the United States, and Mexico. In January 1995, the World Trade Organization (WTO) was created by seventy six nations. In May 1995, one hundred and seventy nations decided to extend the Nuclear Non-Proliferation Treaty indefinitely. In December 1996, a speech by the Federal Reserve Board Chairman, Alan Greenspan, stated that "irrational exuberance" is causing the extraordinary runup of stock prices. Between 1992 and 2000 was the presidency of Bill Clinton. Except for short wars, there was a time of relative peace, economic development, and prosperity. In correspondence with these events, the DJIA grew from about 3000 in 1990 to over 11,000 in 2000.

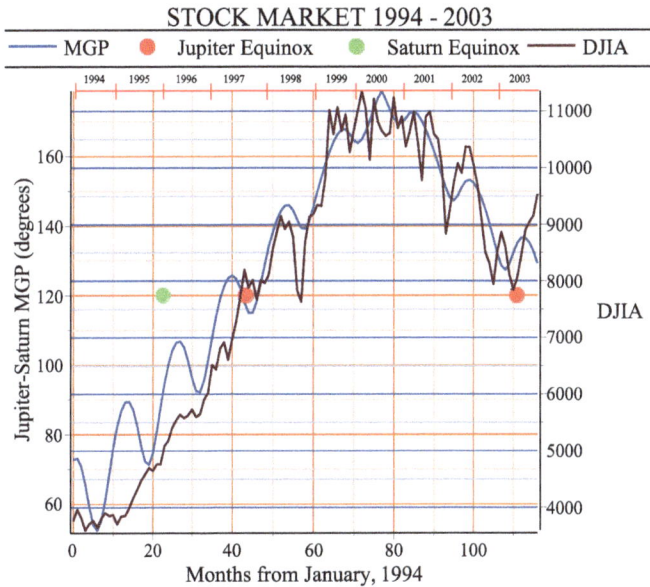

Figure 3.9: Comparison between the DJIA and the Jupiter-Saturn MGP, 1994-2003

In the astronomical environment, the Jupiter-Saturn MGP also grew from about 10 degrees in 1990 to 180 degrees in 2000 (Figure 3.9). To better appreciate this correlation, we present the portion between 1994 and 2003, which includes the market decline of 2000-2003 previously covered. Figure 3.10 shows the statistical cross correlation between the DJIA and the MGP for the period 1994-2003. The correlation coefficient $r=0.97$ or 97%, indicating an excellent agreement. For the whole period of 1990-2003 the correlation coefficient decreases slightly to $r=0.96$.

Figure 3.9 also shows the occurrence of a Saturn equinox in November 1995, which did not seem to affect the DJIA, perhaps because both Saturn's distance to the Sun (9.6 AU), and Jupiter's distance to the Sun (5.3 AU) were close to their *aphelion*. In other words, they were at a point in their orbits which is most distant from the Sun. The further a planet is from the Sun, the less disruptive its influence due to equinoxes.

There was a Jupiter equinox in August, 1997. Its disruptive influence on the stock market was felt only after April, 1998. The DJIA declined from about 9,100 in April 1998 to about 6,800 in September 1998, the only significant decline between 1990 and 2000. Incidently, Jupiter's distance from the Sun decreased from 4.99 AU in April 1998 to about 4.96 AU in September 1998. The latter being very close to the *perihelion*, that is the point in its orbit closest to the Sun. The closer a planet is from the Sun, the more disruptive its influence due to equinoxes. It may be worth mentioning that the distance of Jupiter to the Earth decreased from about 5.5 AU in April 1998 to about 4.0 AU in September 1998, which represents about its minimum value. While there appears to be an influence of a planet's distance to the Sun, we will have to further investigate the effect a planet's distance to the Earth.

CORRELATION MGP-DJIA, 1994 - 2003

Linear Regression ——— 95% Confidence Limits

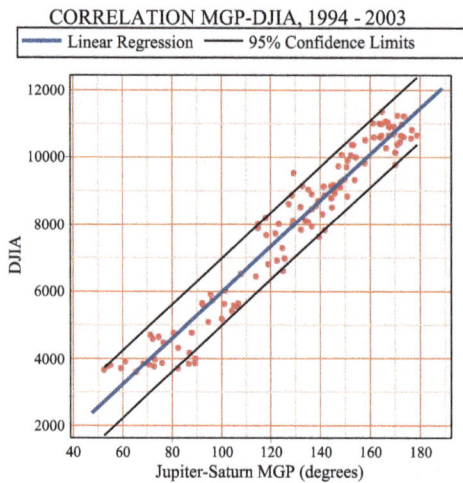

Figure 3.10: Statistical correlation between the Jupiter-Saturn MGP and the DJIA, 1994-2003

It is interesting to see in Figure 3.9 the market decline of 2000-2003 from a larger perspective than that shown in Figure 3.7.

The Market Crash of 1987

The stock market crash known as Black Monday occurred in the New York Stock Exchange on October 19, 1987. The DJIA registered a record 22.6% drop in one day. Stock markets around the world reacted with similar drops of their own.

The stock market crash of 1987 was temporary; for the year of 1987, the DJIA rose a modest 2.26%. The cause of the crash was primarily program trading, used by institutions to protect themselves from significant market weakness. Some secondary factors included excessive valuations, illiquid markets and market psychology.

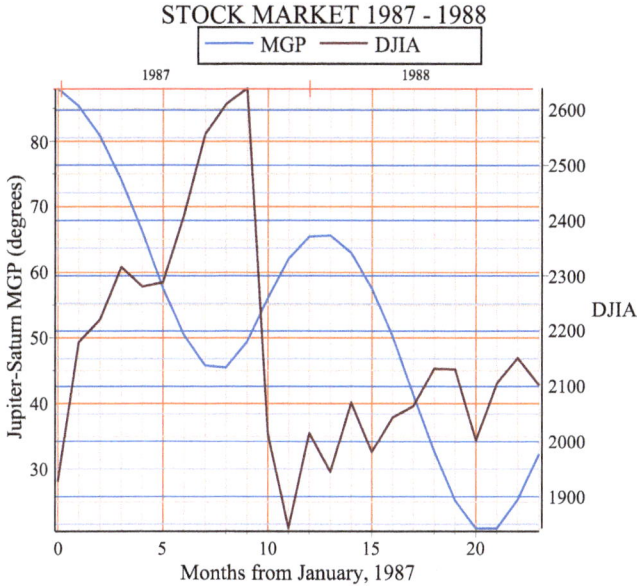

Figure 3.11: Comparison between the DJIA and the Jupiter-Saturn MGP, 1987-1988

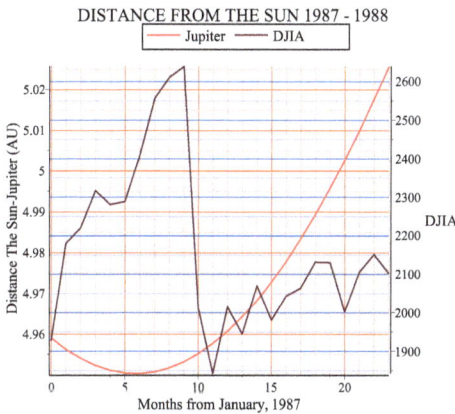

Figure 3.12: Distance the Sun-Jupiter with time

In an attempt to observe astronomical events that may shed light, we first display Figure 3.11 illustrating a comparison between monthly values the DJIA and those of the Jupiter-Saturn MGP for the period 1987-1988. There was an average downward trend in the MGP from about 87 degrees in January 1987 to about 30 degrees by the end of 1988, implying a negative, decreasing, influence on stock prices. In opposition to this influence, however, the DJIA increased from less than 1900 in January 1987 to about 2650 in October 1987. By the end of the same month, the DJIA was a little over 1850. Thus, a downward astronomical influence was only felt in October 1987. There were not planetary equinoxes in the vicinity, except for the Earth's equinox. However, as shown in Figure 3.12, the distance between the Sun and Jupiter reached its minimum of about 4.95 AU (i.e., at perihelion) in June 1987.

DISTANCE FROM THE EARTH 1987 - 1988

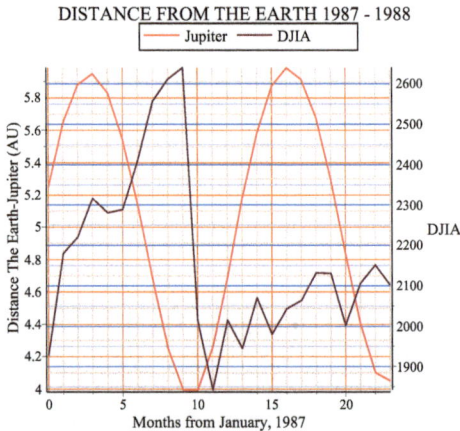

Figure 3.13: Distance the Earth-Jupiter

Additionally, in October 1987 the distance of Jupiter to the Earth was at a minimum of about 4.0 AU (Figure 3.13). Thus, we see that the combined effects of a downward trend in the MGP, a minimum distance between the Sun and Jupiter, and a minimum distance between the Earth and Jupiter resulted in a temporary disruption in the stock market. However, the effects of this anomaly did not occur immediately.

It is interesting to remark that sometimes, the MGP temporarily contradicts the DJIA. We saw this at the beginning of 1987, when a declining MGP opposed a rising DJIA. The effects of a declining MGP did not manifest until late in 1987.

The Variable Market of 1978-1981

In this period, the stock market exhibited short ups and downs between January 1978 and around March 1980, followed by a rally until about February 1981, and a correction at the end of 1981. The Jupiter-Saturn MGP (Figure 3.14) shows an average rising trend until its peak in March 1981. The rising trend is disrupted by the occurrence of a Jupiter equinox in July 1979, and a Saturn equinox in March 1980. The DJIA correction at the end of 1981 coincides with the beginning of a downward trend in the MGP.

A graph of the distance between the Sun and Jupiter (Figure 3.15) shows an increasing separation between the two, thus reinforcing the rising value of the MGP, which again is disrupted by the equinoxes.

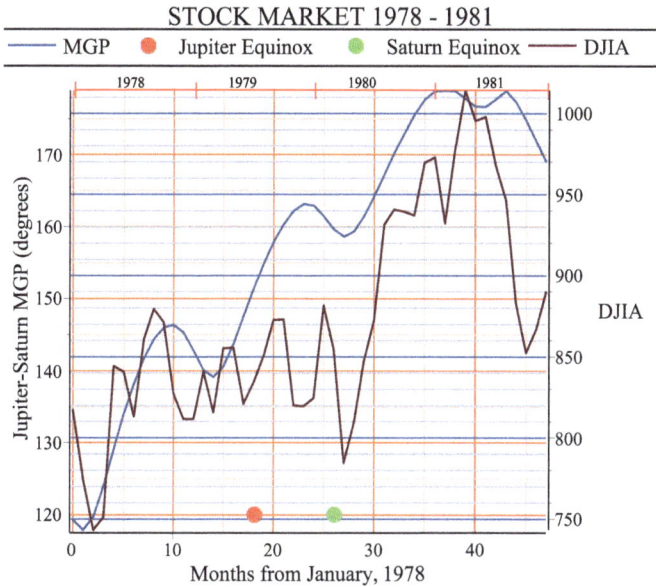

Figure 3.14: Comparison between the DJIA and the Jupiter-Saturn
MGP, 1978-1981

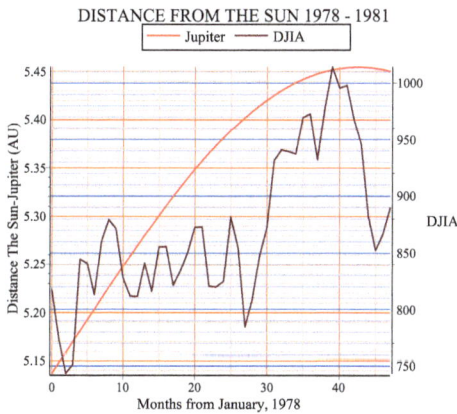

Figure 3.15: Distance the Sun-Jupiter with time

It is illustrative to study a graph of the distance between the Earth and
Jupiter (Figure 3.16), and compare it with the lows in the DJIA. Some of
the lows in the DJIA are near the minimum distances between the Earth
and Jupiter: At 0, 13, 26, and especially the big correction at 39 months
after January 1978, which correspond to January 1978, January 1979,
February 1980, and March 1981, respectively.

DISTANCE FROM THE EARTH 1978 - 1981

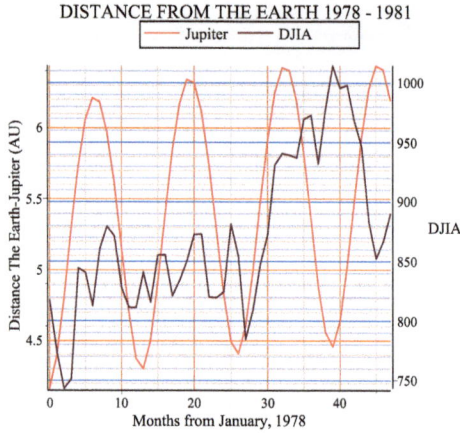

Figure 3.16: Distance the Earth-Jupiter

The Stock Market 1970-1976

This was a time of important political and economic changes. It was the time of the Vietnam War where the U. S. was defeated for the first time. Besides the heavy casualties, the war was a source of profound social opposition and psychological consternation, whose impact still influences American external policy today.

STOCK MARKET 1970 - 1976

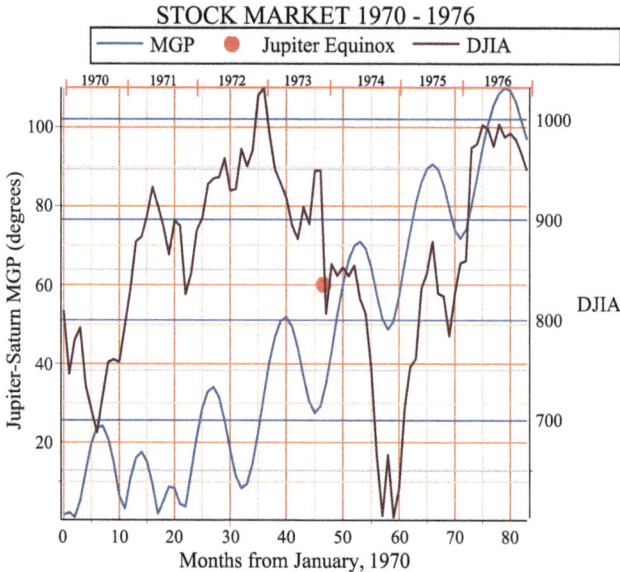

Figure 3.17: Comparison between the DJIA and the Jupiter-Saturn MGP, 1970-1976

At the same time, this was a period of peace initiatives. The year of 1972 saw an unprecedented visit of an American president, Richard Nixon, to China, and the normalization of relationships with the socialist nation. During the same year, Nixon made the first visit of an American president to the Soviet Union, signed a strategic arms pact, and announced the sale of American wheat to the socialist nation. Between 1972 and 1974 was the Watergate political crisis (Emery, 1995), which culminated with the resignation of president Nixon, an unprecedented event. In October 1973, oil imports from Arab oil-producing nations to the U. S. were banned after the start of the Arab-Israeli war, creating a severe energy crisis.

Beyond its typical wavy pattern, the Jupiter-Saturn MGP (Figure 3.17) shows a general rising trend between 0 degrees in January 1970 and about 100 degrees by December 1976. The DJIA coincides with a rise between about 800 in January 1970 and 1,100 in December 1972. However, between December 1972 and November 1974, the DJIA contradicts the MGP by declining from 1,100 to about 600. After November 1974, the DJIA resumes increasing, in agreement with the general rising trend of the MGP.

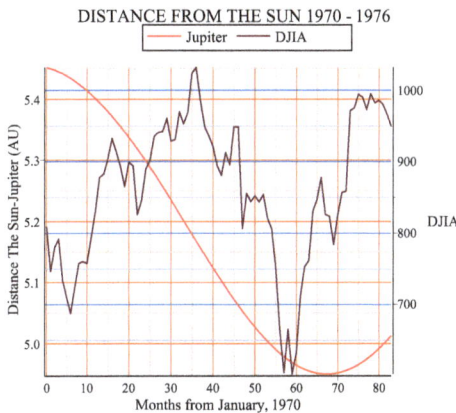

Figure 3.18: Distance the Sun-Jupiter with time

The disruption in the DJIA between 1972 and 1974, which contradicts the rising trend in the MGP, may be partially explained by the occurrence of a Jupiter equinox in November 1973. We can also see that during 1970-1976 Jupiter is approaching the Sun (Figure 3.18), thus increasing the potential disruption to the stock market.

Once again, we note an apparent correspondence between some the low values in the DJIA and the low peaks of the distance between Jupiter and the Earth (Figure 3.19). For instance, we see that some of the low peaks in the DJIA are near some of the low peaks in the Earth-Jupiter distance at 4, 20, 43, 56, and 69 months after January 1970. Interestingly, the minimum distance between the Earth and Jupiter in Figure 3.19 occurred at 69 months, which coincides with the time of the minimum distance between the Sun and Jupiter in Figure 3.18, which also coincides with the time of the minimum value of the DJIA in Figure 3.17 (69 months or November 1974).

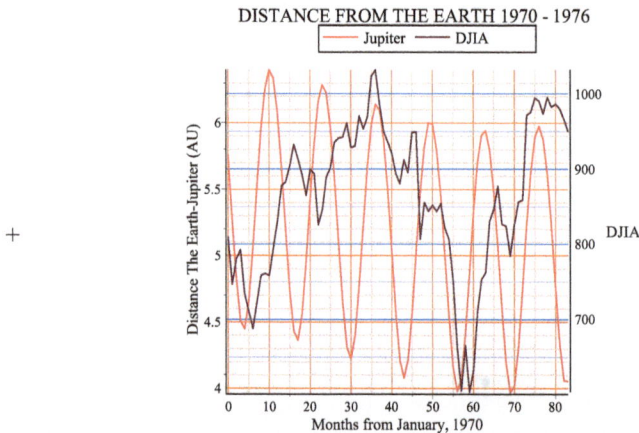

Figure 3.19: Distance the Earth-Jupiter

This phenomenon, which does not always manifest, suggests that a decreasing distance between the Sun and Jupiter, or a decreasing distance between the Earth and Jupiter may have a disruptive, downward, effect on the stock market. We may also conclude that any disruptive effect on the general MGP prevents the possibility of a linear cross correlation between the latter and the DJIA.

The Stock Market 1965-1970

This was the time of the Vietnam War, and the civil rights movement. There was unrest and violence, including the Watts riots in Los Angeles (1965), the riots in Newark, the 12th Street riots in Detroit (1967) with many casualties, injuries, and the destruction of property. Martin Luther King, a prominent civil rights leader, was assassinated in 1968. The Alcatraz Island was occupied by fourteen American Indians in a long standoff over the issues of Indian causes. There was also some positive peace initiatives, such as the summit between President Lyndon B. Johnson and Soviet Premier Alexei Kosygin.

In 1969, the first American astronauts landed on the Moon, and the Internet was invented by the U. S. Department of Defense. In the 1960s the U. S. experienced a long economic expansion. The housing and computer industries surpassed automobiles, chemicals, and electrically powered consumer durables, which were the leading sectors in the 1950s.

Figure 3.20 shows the DJIA and the MGP during 1965-1970. The DJIA had two rallies: from January to December 1965, and from January 1967 to November 1968. During the first rally, the DJIA rose from about 870 to 970, and in the second, from 760 to 980, respectively. There were two important drops: from January to December 1966, and from

November 1968 to June 1970. In the first, the DJIA fell from about 970 to 760, and in the second from 980 to 690, respectively. On the other hand, the MGP shows an average downward trend, from about 100 degrees in January 1965 to 5 degrees in December 1970.

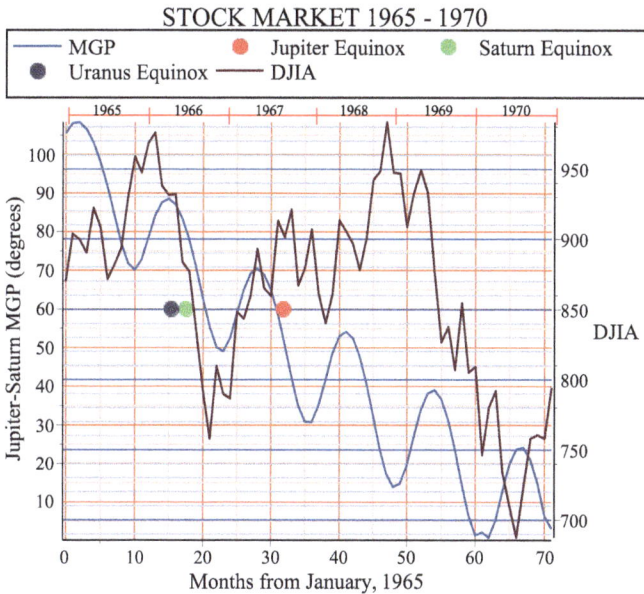

Figure 3.20: Comparison between the DJIA and the Jupiter-Saturn MGP, 1965-1970

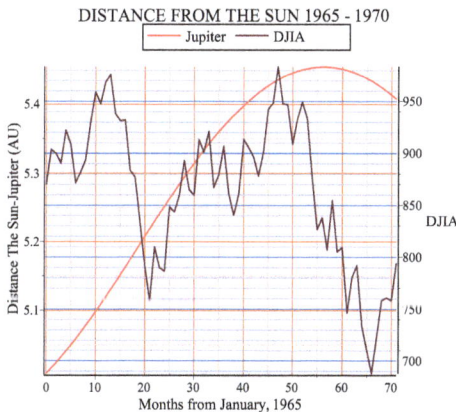

Figure 3.21: Distance the Sun Jupiter

There were three planetary equinoxes during this time: A Uranus equinox in January 1966, a Saturn equinox in June 1966, and a Jupiter equinox in August 1967. The first two seem to accentuate the downward trend in the MGP, thus creating the first drop. However, the third equinox does not seem to have a negative effect on the market, except for a small drop in the Fall of 1967. On the contrary, the DJIA rises to produce the second rally. A clue as to why the Jupiter equinox did not seem to have its usual disruptive effect on the market is provided by observing the evolution of the planet's distance to the Sun. Figure 3.21 shows a continuous increase in this distance during the entire period 1965-1970. An increasing distance form the Sun tends to ameliorate the effect of the planet's MGP and its equinox on the Earth.

The Bull Market of 1950-1962

The 1950s was a time of vigorous economic development, unprecedented growth in productivity, a demographic explosion, a dramatic increase in government spending, the construction of many interstate highways and schools, an extraordinary increase in military spending in new airplanes and new technologies like computers. Unemployment and inflation were low, and there was a sense of prosperity and well being.

At the same time, there were many conflicts. During the 1950s, the civil rights movement, the struggle against racism and segregation, entered the mainstream of American life. There were many protests, boycotts, and acts of nonviolent resistance that shaped the civil rights movement of the 1960s.

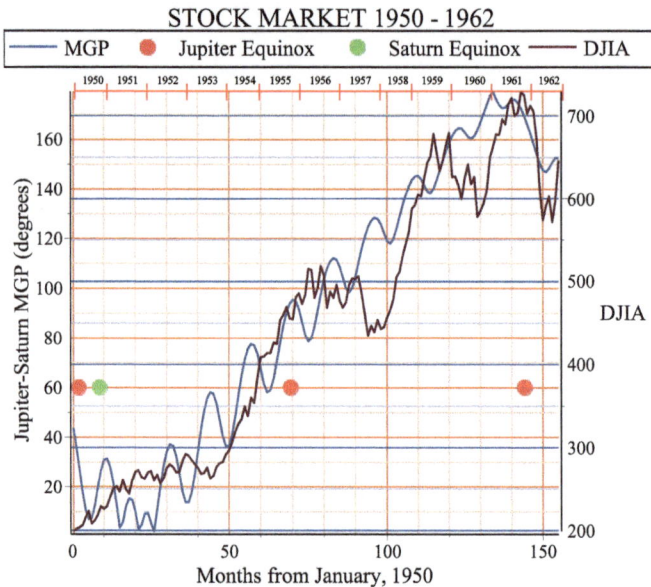

Figure 3.22: Comparison between the DJIA and the Jupiter-Saturn MGP, 1950-1962

This was the time of the Korean War (1950-1953), the Vietnam War (1955-1975), and the Cold War. The latter manifested as a growing tension between the U. S. and the Soviet Union, which was regarded as an expansive socialist empire, and a threat to democracy. This fight against communism also took the form of repression against dissent and "subversion" inside the country.

As shown in Figure 3.22, the MGP rose from about 20 degrees at the beginning of 1950 to a peak of almost 165 degrees towards the end of 1962. In agreement with this upward trend in the MGP, the DJIA increased from about 200 to about 720 during the same interval. A Jupiter equinox in February 1950, and a Saturn equinox in September 1950 do not seem to disrupt the future MGP upward trend, but rather the market downward trend of prior months in 1949 (not shown).

There was a second Jupiter equinox in October 1955, which again does not seem to have any effect on the market, possibly because Jupiter was 5.35 AU from the Sun –near its aphelion. As described before, the further the distance from the Sun, the lesser its influence. There was a third Jupiter equinox in January 1960 –about 150 months from January 1950–, when Jupiter was about 5.0 AU from the Sun –near its perihelion. These seem closely associated with a drop in the DJIA from 720 to about 570 in the following months.

I cannot find any astronomical event associated with a temporary, but noticeable, market drop in September 1957 –about 93 months after January 1950. Other non-astronomical events may be the reason: In September 1957, Arkansas Governor Orval Faubus activated the National Guard to bar nine black students from attending previously all-white Central High School in Little Rock, Arkansas. He withdrew the troops on September 21 and the students were allowed entrance to class two days later. A threat of violence caused President Eisenhower to dispatch federal troops to Little Rock on September 24 to enforce the edict. Investors dislike uncertainty and violence, and certainly this was a time with a potential for both.

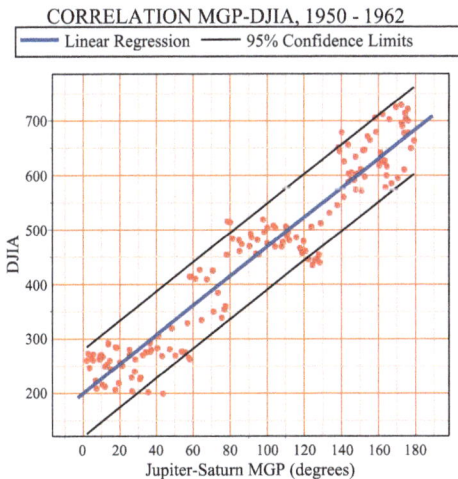

Figure 3.23: Correlation between the Jupiter-
Saturn MGP and the DJIA, 1950-1962

In spite of these short time exceptions, the overall correspondence between the DJIA and the MGP during this period 1950-1962 is remarkable. Figure 3.23 shows a statistical cross correlation between the MGP and the DJIA. The correlation coefficient is r=0.96 or 96%, which is excellent.

From the historical examples we have seen so far, we observe that during periods of a general increase in the MGP, the DJIA also seems to grow in direct correlation with the former, unless some disruptive astronomical events occur that perturb or even reverse its growth influence. The occurrence of a planetary equinox is an example of such a disturbance. The effect of this event is enhanced or ameliorated by the distance between the planet and the Sun, and/or its distance to the Earth. A decreasing distance tends to accentuate the disruptive effect on the market, and an increasing distance tends to mitigate such a negative effect. We have also found that there are times when no astronomical event explains a temporary disruption in the market. In those cases the reasons are strictly economical or political in nature.

The Market of 1943-1949

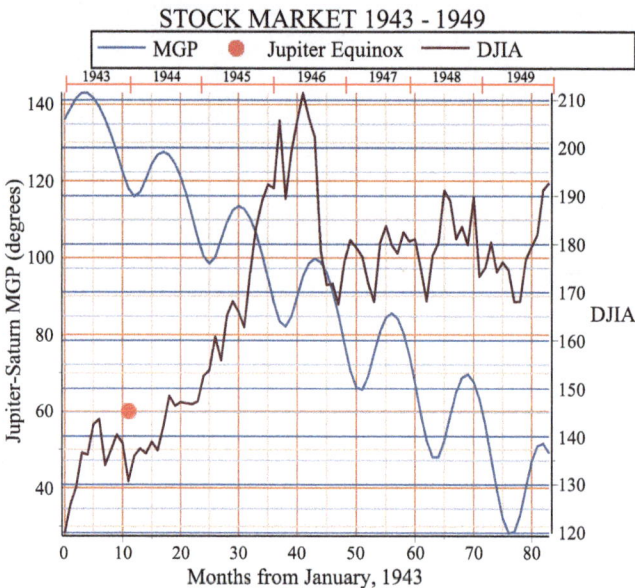

Figure 3.24: Comparison between the DJIA and the Jupiter-Saturn MGP, 1943-1949

This time was the second phase of World War II, which included the invasion of Europe by allied troops (1944), the surrender of Germany (1945), the detonation of the atomic bombs in Hiroshima and Nagasaki, Japan (1945), followed by the surrender of Japan. Between 1945 and 1949 was the reconstruction of Europe, the United Nations was formed by fifty one nations (1946), the Organization of American States was founded (1948), and the North American Treaty Organization, was formed by the United States, Canada, and ten Western European nations (1949).

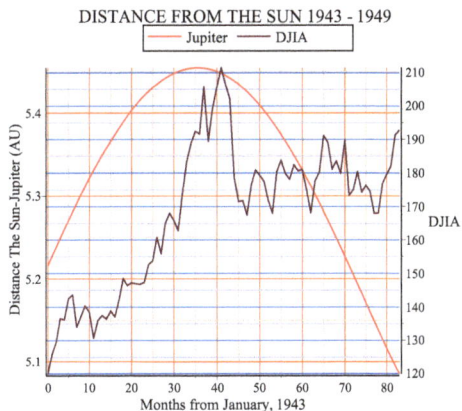

Figure 3.25: Distance the Sun-Jupiter

Here we have an example when astronomical influences seem to contradict the actual market performance (Figure 3.24). The Jupiter-Saturn MGP exhibits a declining trend from 140 degrees to about 50 from 1943 to 1949. However, the DJIA actually rises from 120 in January 1943 to about 210 in June 1946. A Jupiter equinox in December 1943 only caused a small drop. During this time, the market was recovering from its previous losses in 1942 (see Figure 3.26, next section). It is only after June 1946 that the downward trend of the MGP showed an affect on the market, beginning with a drastic correction in July 1946. After that, the DJIA jumped up and down around an average of 175. Thus, a downward trend in the MGP did not affect the market during the first half of this period, and during the second half the actual drop in the market was partial.

One explanation of this anomaly is the distance between Jupiter and the Sun, which increased during the first half of this period –thus decreasing the influence of the planet on the market. The distance reached its aphelion in December 1946, and decreased during the second half (Figure 3.25). We may also add that the market seems to have a greater receptivity to a generally rising MGP than a falling one. In other words, prolonged periods of a rising MGP appear to coincide with prolonged periods of a bull market, whereas prolonged periods of a declining MGP only partially or intermittently coincide with a bear market.

The Market of 1939-1942

World War II began in 1939, but the U. S. did not enter officially until the end of 1941, after Japan attacked Pearl Harbor. The most important events in 1942 were war related: Japanese Americans were confined in relocation camps in the West Coast; the U. S. was victorious in the Battle of Midway against the Japanese fleet; the U. S. invaded the Solomon Islands in the Pacific and North Africa; the development of the first atomic bomb began.

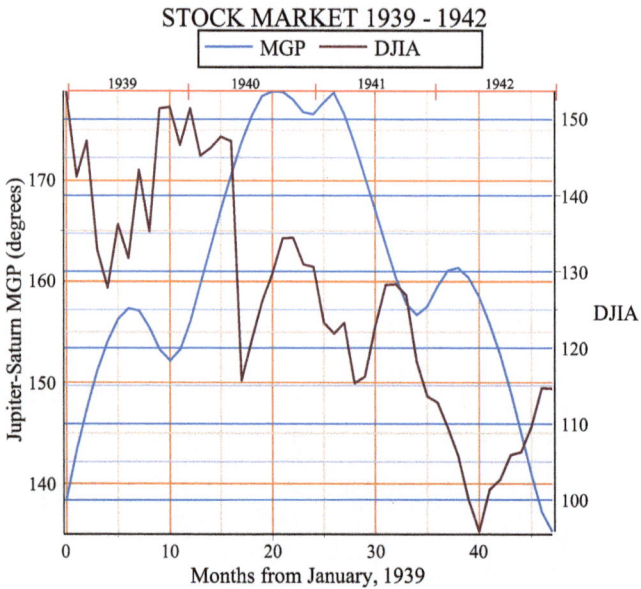

Figure 3.26: Comparison between the DJIA and the Jupiter-Saturn MGP, 1939-1942

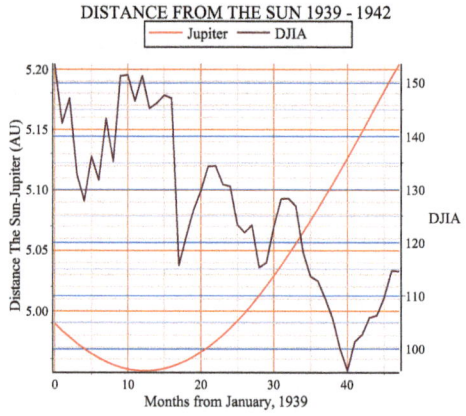

Figure 3.27: Distance The Sun-Jupiter

As shown in Figure 3.26, the MGP continued to increase from the prior years (see Figure 3.28, next section) until it reached its peak around August 1940, and then started its descending cycle. In concert with this, the DJIA continued its rise observed from the prior years (see Figure 3.28, next section), reaching a peak of about 150 in October 1939, and then began a descending pattern, characterized by some abrupt drops, until it reached a low of about 95 in April 1942. One important drop occurred in April 1940, which coincided with Jupiter being near its perihelion (Figure 3.27).

The Bull Market of 1932-1938

During this period, the U. S. was struggling to overcome the sequels of the Great Depression and to reestablish economic growth and investors confidence. The unemployment rate in 1932 reached about 24.9%. Several measures were enacted to stimulate growth. The Reconstruction Finance Corporation was established to stimulate banking and business in 1932. President Franklin D. Roosevelt was inaugurated in 1933. The New Deal social and economic programs were passed by the United States Congress in 1933 to address depression era economics. The U. S. Securities and Exchange Commission was established in 1934. The Social Security Act was passed by Congress in 1935. Many infrastructure projects were inaugurated, such as roads, railroads, bridges.

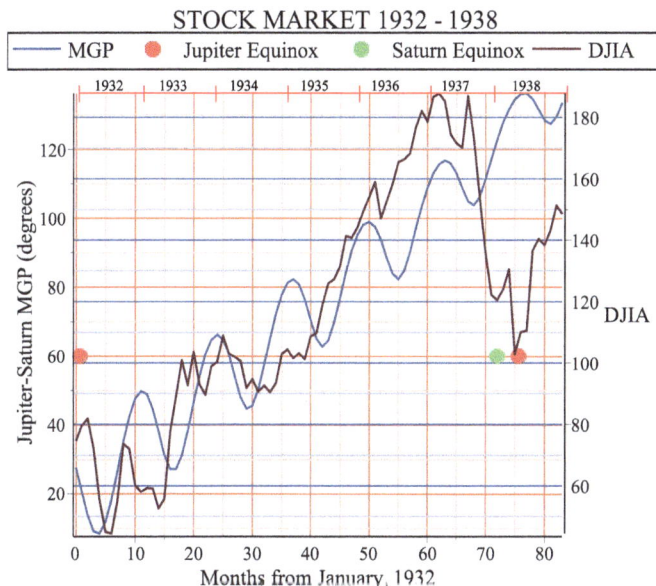

Figure 3.28: Comparison between the DJIA and the Jupiter-Saturn MGP, 1932-1938

This was also the time of the rise of Adolf Hitler in Nazi's Germany (1933), The Great Terror began in the Soviet Union (1934), and Mao Tse-tung began the Long March in China (1934). It was a period of relative peace and growth, but the world was preparing for a second great war.

These events reflected on a continued rise in the DJIA, from about 80 in February 1932 to 185 in July 1937 (Figure 3.28), followed by a substantial drop to 105 in March 1938. Corresponding with the rise in the

DJIA during the same interval, there was a rise in the MGP from about 30 degrees in January 1932 to about 105 in July 1937. However, the MGP continued to rise to about 130 in December 1938. We may blame the drop in the DJIA between July 1937 and March 1938 on the occurrence of a Saturn equinox in December 1937, and a Jupiter equinox in April 1938. Also, there was a Jupiter equinox in January 1932, which accounts for a large correction in the DJIA in earlier months (not shown).

A cross correlation between the MGP and the DJIA shows a calculated correlation coefficient $r=0.76$. This value would have been much higher had it not been for the equinox anomaly.

The Great Depression of 1929-1932

The Great Depression started in 1929, culminating a decade of optimism, lavish spending, and a booming stock market. People believed they could make a fortune from the stock market and invested their life savings. Many bought stocks on margin –buying stocks by borrowing 80% of the value of the stock. This mass hysteria caused many companies to invest and also banks to invest customer's money in the market.

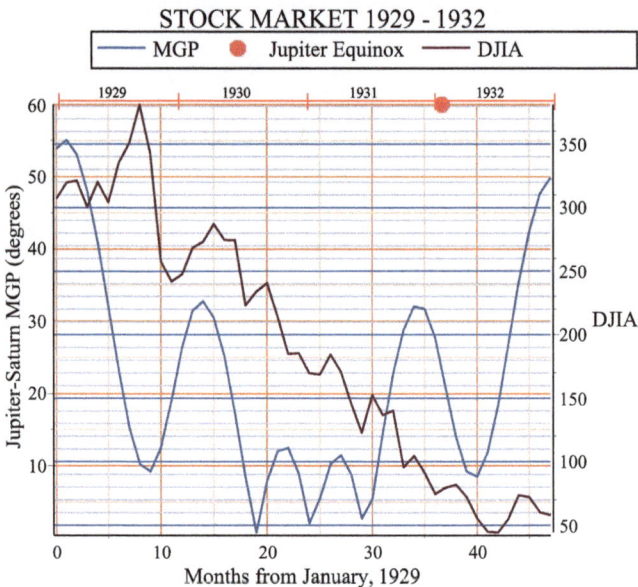

Figure 3.29: Comparison between the DJIA and the Jupiter-Saturn MGP, 1929-1932

In October 1929, the market began to collapse, setting a chain reaction that propagated through the entire economy. Everyone wanted to sell, but no one was buying, causing shares to further drop in value; banks closed, people in panic rushed to withdraw their deposits from the remaining banks, causing them to close. Many companies went bankrupt and unemployment soared. At the same time, a severe drought in the Midwest ruined many farmers. The DJIA lost 17.17% in 1929, 33.77% in 1930, 52.57% in 1931, and 23.07% in 1932. From the peak of about 380 in September 1929, the DJIA came down to about 60 in December 1932 (Figure 3.29). Prior to 1929, the MGP was declining, concluding with a minimum of 0 degrees in December 1930 –Jupiter in opposition to Saturn–, after which if began its next rising cycle, which did not seem to help the DJIA recover due to a disruptive Jupiter equinox in January 1932. It is interesting to note that in January 1929 Jupiter was at perihelion (7.98 AU).

The Market of 1925-1928

We briefly study this period as another example of a case when the DJIA increases in value in spite of a downward influence of the MGP. This substantiates the idea that a rising MGP tends to correlate better with a rising DJIA than a declining one. Although the effects of a downward MGP will be eventually observed in the market, sometimes market forces seem to ignore this for a while. Figure 3.30 illustrates this. The MGP declines from 130 degrees to about 50 degrees between 1925 and 1928. The market exuberance and investors frenzy appear to ignore its effects. During the same period, the DJIA rose from 120 to 290, and this in spite of a Jupiter equinox in June 1926, which made a minor dent in the stock prices. As shown in Figure 3.29, the effects of the declining MGP were only felt in 1929 and in 1930, when it reached its minimum – Jupiter in opposition to Saturn– in the midst of the Great depression.

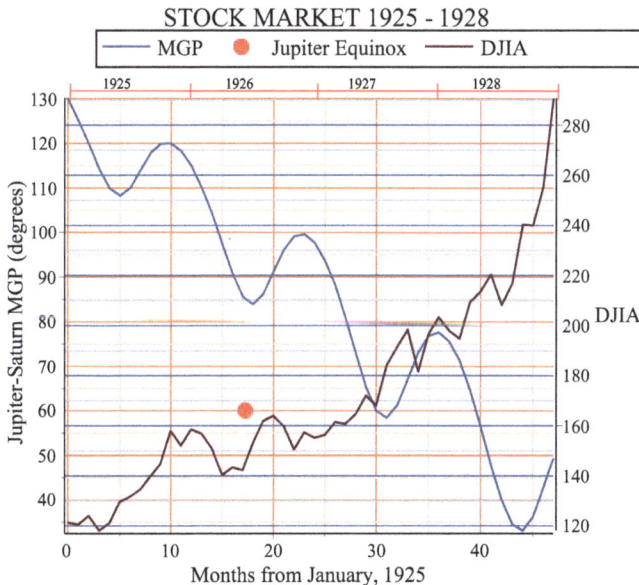

Figure 3.30: Comparison between the DJIA and the Jupiter-Saturn MGP, 1925-1928

The Market of 1910-1924

This was a tumultuous period characterized by wars and conflicts. The most important war was World war I, one of the most brutal and devastating conflicts in history (1914-1918). The war caused the abdication of various monarchies and the collapse of five of the last modern empires of Russia, Germany, China, Ottoman Turkey and Austria-Hungary –divided into Austria, Hungary, southern Poland, Czechoslovakia and Yugoslavia. Other important wars during the decade were: The Wadai War (1909–1911) between France and the Ouaddai Kingdom, Africa; the Italo-Turkish War (1911–1912); the First Balkan Wars (1912–1913); the Saudi-Ottoman War (1913); the Latvian War of Independence (1918-1920) against Russia.

The decade of the 1910s was also a period of internal conflicts and revolutions in several countries: The Mexican Revolution (1910); the Russian Revolution (1917) and the establishment of communism; the Armenian Genocide in Turkey (1915-1920); The Jallianwala Bagh massacre in India (1919), which led to the Indian Independence from Britain; the Xinhai Revolution, which caused the overthrow of China's ruling Qing Dynasty, and the establishment of the Republic of China (1912-1949).

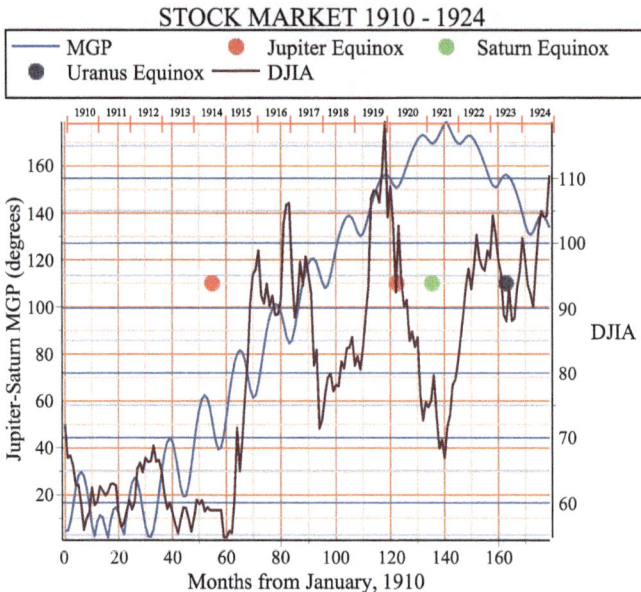

Figure 3.31: Comparison between the DJIA and the Jupiter-Saturn MGP, 1910-1924

A graph of the MGP and the DJIA during 1910-1924 is shown in Figure 3.31. The MGP has a minimum of 0 degrees around December 1910 —Jupiter is in opposition to Saturn–, after which begins its rising cycle, culminating with a peak value of 180 degrees in October 1921, followed by the next descending cycle. In agreement with this, the DJIA exhibits a general rising trend with some notable exceptions. First, there is a disruption due to a Jupiter equinox in July 1914. In the second exception to the general rising trend in the MGP, the DJIA falls from 106 to 72 between January and November 1917. There are no astronomical events explaining this drop. However, we should remember that during this time the U. S. officially entered World War I; investors dislike conflicts and uncertainty. In the third exception to the general rising trend in the MGP, the DJIA falls from about 118 to 65 between October 1919 and August, 1921 which coincides with a Jupiter equinox in March 1920, and a Saturn equinox in April 1921. We should also notice another fall in the DJIA between February and October 1923, which is near a Uranus equinox in December 1923.

The Market of 1900-1910

The first decade of the 20th century resembled the 19th century that had just ended. The main changes of the new century began to occur after 1910. However, there were inventions and contributions to science and technology that impacted the decades that followed: Max Planck formulated the Quantum Theory in physics (1900); Sigmund Freud published "The Interpretation of Dreams," setting the stage for modern psychology with the discovery of the unconscious (1900); Kodak introduced the Brownie cameras (1900); Guglielmo Marconi broadcast the first transatlantic radio signal (1901); Wilbur and Orville Wright succeeded in the first sustained and manned plane flight (1903); Albert Einstein published the theory of special relativity (1905), transforming theoretical physics and astronomy during the 20th century; the first successful field tractor is invented by Benjamin Holt (1904); the first passenger flight on a plane occurs at Huffman Prairie Flying Field in Dayton, Ohio (1908); the first production Model T car is built at the Ford plant in Detroit, Michigan (1908).

From the financial point of view, October 1907 witnessed The Panic of 1907. It was the first worldwide financial crisis of the 20th century. It transformed a recession into a depression surpassed in severity only by the Great Depression. Its effects are still felt today, because it produced the monetary reform movement that led to the establishment of the Federal Reserve System.

As shown in Figure 3.32, the MGP started its descending cycle in October 1901, and gradually decreased until the end of 1909. Parallel to the MGP, the DJIA had a peak of about 56 around July 1901, and declined to about 36 in December 1903. This decline was partially encouraged by a Jupiter equinox in September 1902. We should also remember that in September 1901 President William H. McKinley was assassinated at the Pan-American Exposition in Buffalo, NY. Markets dislike political instability.

As shown in Figure 3.32, the MGP started its descending cycle in October 1901, and gradually decreased until the end of 1909. Parallel to the MGP, the DJIA had a peak of about 56 around July 1901, and declined to about 36 in December 1903. This decline was partially encouraged by a Jupiter equinox in September 1902. We should also remember that in September 1901 President William H. McKinley was assassinated at the Pan-American Exposition in Buffalo, NY. Markets dislike political instability.

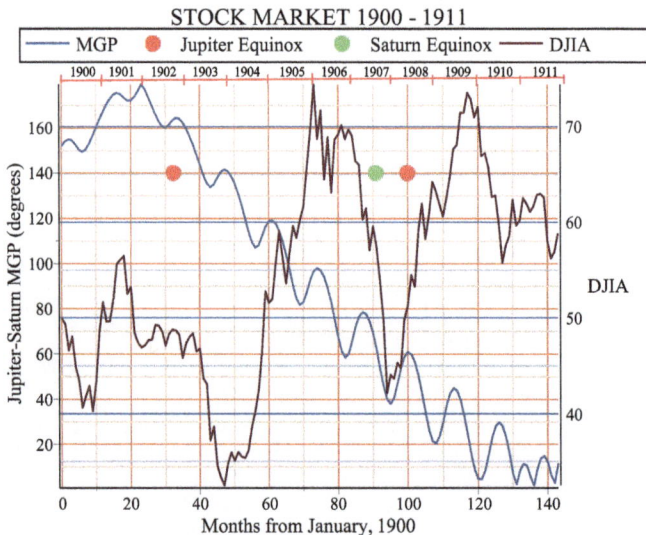

Figure 3.32: Comparison between the DJIA and the Jupiter-Saturn MGP, 1900-1911

After December 1903, the DJIA recovers and rises, in opposition to a declining MGP, until it reaches a peak of about 74 in February 1906. Then it declines unsteadily until about 42 in November 1907. Recall that in October 1907 was The Panic of 1907. It is interesting to note that these events coincide with a Saturn equinox in July 1907, and it is near a Jupiter equinox in April 1908. After November 1907, the DJIA recovers, again in opposition to a declining MGP until it reaches about 73 in October, 1909. Then, it declines to 56 in August 1910 and remains around this value for a few months, in agreement with a minimum value in the MGP.

Conclusions of the Study

In this chapter, we conducted an investigation of the effect of astronomical conditions on stock market indices. Specifically, we studied a relationship between astronomical positions of the planets in the solar system and the DJIA. The astronomical positions of individual planets, as well as the relative positions of two planets, were compared to the value of the DJIA on the first trading day of each month for the period from 1900 to 2020. When two planets were considered, the following combinations were studied: Venus-Mars, Venus-Jupiter, Venus-Saturn, Mars-Jupiter, Jupiter-Saturn, Jupiter-Uranus, Jupiter-Neptune. The effect of three or more planets was not studied at this time. We also investigated the possible effect of other planetary phenomena, such as the occurrence of planetary equinoxes and the effect of their distance to the Sun or the Earth.

We were seeking a relationship between environmental astronomy and the DJIA that manifests over intermediate periods lasting months to years. We believe such intervals render better opportunities for portfolio planning. Consistent with these objectives, astronomical cycles of the order of days or weeks were not considered. Such cycles would be more appropriate for day trading and were left out of this study.

The results of this research may be summarized as follows:

1. At the scale of months, the astronomical position of a planet relative to another –the angular distance between them– appears to be more important in its effect on the market than the planet's individual position in geocentric or ecliptic coordinates.

2. The angular distance between two planets $-\theta$ as observed from the Earth in sexagesimal degrees– has an inverse relationship with the DJIA. As this distance increases to a maximum of 180 degrees –when the planets are in opposition–, the DJIA tends to decrease. Conversely, as the angular distance decreases to a minimum of zero –when the planets are in conjunction– the DJIA tends to increase. We defined the Market Growth potential (MGP) as the supplementary angle to the angular distance, $MGP=180-\theta$. Then, as the MGP increases, the DJIA tends to increase, and the MGP decreases, the DJIA tends to decrease as well.

3. At the scale of months, the MGP of the large outer planets in the solar system –Jupiter, Saturn, Uranus, and Neptune– appear to be more important cycles in their effect on the market than those of the smaller or inner planets –Mercury, Venus, Mars. The most important cycle is the Jupiter-Saturn MGP with a synodic period of 19.87 years between peak to peak –between two successive conjunctions. The MGP increases during 9.94 years –19.87/2–, and decreases during the following 9.94 years. The cycles of other planet combinations –Jupiter-Uranus, Jupiter-Neptune, Saturn-Uranus, Saturn-Neptune–, have synodic periods of several decades. We do not have DJIA historical data long enough to ascertain a statistical correlation. Future research should be devoted to them.

4. The rising cycle in the Jupiter-Saturn MGP tends to have a better affinity with a correspondingly rising DJIA. Several rising cycles exhibited excellent linear cross-correlation between the two signals. This makes it easier to forecast a bull market.

5. However, a declining MGP cycle sometimes shows marked differences with the behavior of the DJIA. Sometimes the DJIA drops fast, as compared to a gradual decline in the MGP, and a statistical relationship is poor. Other times the DJIA rises in opposition to a

decreasing MGP, and the effects of a declining MGP are only felt abruptly towards the end of the cycle. This makes the prediction of a bear market difficult, except for favorable conditions for its occurrence.

6. The occurrence of planetary equinoxes, particularly those of the large outer planets –Jupiter and Saturn–, appear to have a disruptive effect on the market. Most of the time, they were found to be associated with bear markets. Sometimes an equinox temporarily reverses the effect of a rising MGP. Sometimes it accentuates the effect of a declining MGP.

7. At the scale of hours or days, a single planet's astronomical position may generate short term variations in the stock market. Likewise, combinations of two planets, with one of them or both being a small or inner planet –Venus-Mars, Venus-Jupiter, Venus-Saturn, Mars-Jupiter–, also generate short term variations. Lastly, because of the Earth's revolution around the Sun, the angular distance between the Sun and Jupiter or the Sun and Saturn generate cycles of about one year. Their effect on the market is inconclusive. These shorter cycles should be studied in the future.

8. The distance of a planet to the Sun in AU appears to be more important in its effect on the market than its distance to the Earth. As a planet's distance to the Sun decreases in its elliptical orbit to a minimum at perihelion, the effects of other prevailing astronomical conditions –the effect of the MGP, the occurrence of planetary equinoxes– seem enhanced. As a planet's distance to the Sun increases to a maximum at aphelion, the effect of other astronomical conditions seem mitigated. In either case, the effects of distance not always manifest and the results need further study.

Building equity is not more meritorious than preserving it. In the former, chance plays a big part; in the latter, skill is everything.

Publius Ovidius Naso (43 BC - 17 CE).

When wealth only is lost, nothing of real value is lost, for if one has health and skill one can still be happy and can make more money; but if health is lost, then most happiness is also lost; and when contact with the Principle of life is lost, all happiness and all health are lost.

Paramahansa Yogananda (1893 - 1952).

4 APPLICATIONS TO MARKET FORECASTING AND PORTFOLIO MANAGEMENT

Model Verification versus Model Validation

In Chapter 3, I reported the results of an investigation of the effect of the Earth's astronomical environment on market indices, such as the DJIA. It was stated that certain recurring astronomical features in the solar system may have a correlation with the value of the DJIA, and its evolution over time. The features studied included the astronomical position of the planets in the solar system as observed from the Earth in geocentric or ecliptic coordinates; the angular distance between two planets; the distance of planets to the Earth and to the Sun; and the occurrence of planetary equinoxes as they revolve around the Sun. These features were simulated using standard celestial mechanics formulae at the beginning of each month, and compared to the value of the DJIA for the historical records from 1900 to 2020.

The objective was to identify a cyclical relationship between astronomical characteristics and corresponding trends in the DJIA. Several cycles were identified that appear to have a statistical correlation with the market during certain periods. I focused mainly on cycles of intermediate length of the order of months to a few years in length, rather than those of short-term duration of the order of days to a few weeks, or those of longer duration of the order of decades to centuries in duration. Short-term cycles appear to be of interest to day traders and were left out of this study. Cycles of intermediate duration appear to be of interest to my target audience: the conscientious investor who plans a long-term portfolio management. Cycles of long-term duration cannot be studied as yet, due to the lack of historical market data to verify their existence.

Chapter 3, concluded the *verification* phase of the intermediate-term cycles with 120 years of market data. Several cycles were eliminated from the study, either because they conformed to short-term or long-term duration, or because they did not appear to have a relationship with the DJIA that could be replicated. One cycle appears to have an important relationship with the DJIA: The Jupiter-Saturn angular distance. I defined the Market Growth Potential –MGP in sexagesimal degrees– as the supplementary angle of the distance between two planets. Using the MGP as defined, it is easy to observe that as the MGP increases, the DJIA also tends to increase. The opposite is also true.

Other cycles defined as functions of the angular distance between the larger outer planets were found to have a relationship with the market. However, these cycles are of the order of several decades and we will need to collect market data for centuries to come to identify their features.

The Jupiter-Saturn MGP increases during 9.94 years to a peak of 180 degrees when the two planets are in conjunction, and then decreases during an equal interval of 9.94 years to a value of zero degrees when the two planets are in opposition, as observed from the Earth. This makes a cycle with period of 19.87 years –9.94×2– in duration from peak to peak, or from low to low. Because the rising and descending portions of the cycle are of equal duration –symmetric about the peak–, the MGP has a better affinity to bull markets, when both signals gradually rise, than to bear markets when the DJIA may fall via short-term drops, followed by short-term recoveries. Sometimes a descending MGP cycle contradicts an intriguingly rising DJIA, and the diminishing effects of the MGP are only felt towards the end of the cycle. Thus, I found that sometimes a rising portion of the MGP cycle exhibited an excellent linear statistical correlation with the DJIA. Sometimes the correlation coefficient was as high as 97%. However, poor linear correlation was found in several of the descending cycles in the MGP.

Other astronomical events found to relate to the DJIA in a complex manner included the occurrence of planetary equinoxes, and the distance of the larger planets to the Sun and to the Earth. Just like in the Earth, an equinox is the moment when the celestial equator of a planet crosses the Sun's equator. At that moment, the days and nights are of equal duration. Generally, I found that the interval of time around the occurrence of an equinox is associated with sharp declines in the stock market. This interval may be as long as a few months prior or after the time of the equinox.

Planetary equinoxes were found to disrupt the market. Sometimes when the MGP was increasing, the DJIA was observed to inexplicably drop, except for the occurrence of an equinox around the same time. On the other hand, equinoxes were found to accentuate or accelerate the downward trend of a declining MGP. This disruption and reversal of a rising MGP, or the acceleration and enhancement of a downward MGP, were found to be more important with the equinoxes of the large outer planet, especially Jupiter's and Saturn's. I should remark that these observations concerning the effect of planetary equinoxes are preliminary and need to be further studied. This is so because the number of observed equinoxes over the past century is relatively small and they might not be representative.

Additionally, I found that the distance of one of the larger planets to the Sun, and to a lesser extent to the Earth, tends to increase or decrease the effects of the MGP and those of the equinoxes. For instance, as Jupiter gets closer to the Sun in its elliptical orbit, the effects of a declining MGP tend to increase, and the effects of a rising MGP tend to decrease or be attenuated. For these reasons, I believe that the closer the distance to the Sun the more disruptive its effect on the market. However, at this point further research is necessary because I did not have sufficient events to confirm this observation.

The relationship between astronomical events and the DJIA, as described in this study, does not imply a cause and effect phenomenon. The results of my investigation suggest a quantitative correlation between the two. However, we do not know for certain if the astronomical environment generates unknown phenomena which in turn influences a collective unconscious behavior among investors. All we can state at this time, is that the astronomical environment and the market indices have a relationship –statistical or otherwise functional–, with unknown laws to be identified beyond the basic principles described above. In Chapter 1, we discussed some possible explanations for this relationship, including beliefs held about the underlying forces that cause this phenomenon. These beliefs are part of traditional folklore, astrology –as oppose of astronomy–, ancient mysticism, and cultural philosophy. While they provide a motivation and a rationalization of this relationship, they do not offer a scientific proof. Yet, this does not mean that traditional explanations are wrong. On the contrary, they provide the motivation and hypothetical bases to conduct studies such as this one. Furthermore, from the present study, many of the propositions held in traditional astrology, for example, appear to be correct in their assessment.

Having studied the basic principles of the MGP –with its associated phenomena and limitations–, can we use them to predict the future values of the DJIA? Nothing prevents us from trying. During the *verification* phase of this study –Chapter 3–, I compared calculated astronomical positions with historical market data. Astronomical calculations from standard celestial mechanics are fairly accurate. Of course, I used some approximations –not all of the terms in Kepler's equations–, but the results are precise for my purposes. Likewise, using these equations to predict future astronomical positions and phenomena will produce accurate data. However, we will have to wait years to see how my predictions compare to the market numbers actually recorded. This is the *validation* phase of a model.

In every scientific study, the verification phase that compares with existing data is the easy part of modeling. The trial-by-fire of any science model is the validation with future data. I have spent thirty five years developing mathematical models in science and engineering. In many occasions, a well-verified model validates well with new data, that is within certain acceptable statistical errors. In some occasions, however, poor results of a validation process send the researcher back to the lab or the mathematical analysis needed to improve the model.

For these reasons, a large portion of mathematical models are never validated, and this is true regardless of the scientific field in question. This is to say that there are limitations to using historical data as a base to predict future realizations of a phenomenon. What guarantees us that the way the stock market behaved in the past will be similar in the future? We may speculate that the current geopolitical climate may forever alter the way new investors approach the market. The best we can hope for is that the *statistical* properties of past events will replicate in the future, not the actual historical events. At the very least, we certainly hope that the *qualitative* characteristics of market signals will continue to apply under future conditions.

Thus, while the mathematical calculations of future astronomical conditions are accurate and straight forward, how they relate to the DJIA have a certain degree of uncertainty. For instance, a rising MGP calculated into the future, may not end up following the DJIA as nicely as it did in the past. For instance, in past historical events we observed an inherent uncertainty associated with a descending MGP. In future events, this uncertainty may or may not be amplified. For these reasons, I named the MGP a Market Growth *Potential*. That is to say, a rising MGP has the potential to positively affect the market upwards, and a declining MGP has the potential to negatively affect the market downwards. A high or a low MGP may or may not in fact translate into a correspondingly high or a low in the market. There are simply too many other variables not included in the predictions, many of which I recounted in Chapter 3, such as economical conditions, political upheaval, war. These variables affect the market and are unpredictable. Can anyone predict when the next recession will occur? Certainly, economists can predict *the conditions* for the *potential* development of a recession, and not necessarily the timing of its actual occurrence.

With these limitations in sight, we can proceed to forecast the Market Growth Potential in the future. If we are planning to use the forecast as a tool to aid our future investments, we certainly have to apply it with prudence. I believe that the cautious investor may use the forecast with certain provisions that would maximize profits, while minimizing risks.

What Assets to Buy: Portfolio Planning and Management 101

This section is intended for those readers who are thinking about investing in the stock market, or who have rarely done it in the past, except for the traditional employer-based Individual Retirement Account (IRA). If you are an experienced investor, you may safely skip this section, since it is elementary. You may also disagree with some of the suggestions I give here. This is not a book about financial planning or portfolio design and management. However, since we will be discussing the applications of the MGP and other astronomical events to portfolio management, I find it necessary to briefly describe its basic principles for comprehensiveness.

If you are thinking about investing in the stock market, my first advice is to educate yourself. The principles of investing are fairly simple, but you need to learn them carefully to be successful and to avoid some of the common mistakes that may deprive you of your hard-earned investment money. The easy route here is to hire a financial planner and to let her/him make the essential decisions about which asset classes to buy. This is a costly move. A financial planner may charge one to two percent of your portfolio value per year. This may not seem like much when an investor is starting out, but over the long haul it is a significant portion of a portfolio's return. Also, there is the possibility of a conflict of interest. Some planners are motivated to sell expensive assets that bring them high commissions, but which are not necessary in your best interest. Selecting the right planner is crucial. At the very least, a client should always ask the advisor what benefit s/he receives from selling a particular asset.

Unless you are a wealthy individual with complicated investments in private and public enterprises in several countries, I believe the average individual should learn the principles of investing and try them on his/her own. There is increasing evidence suggesting that investors who purchase assets in passively-managed index funds with low-maintenance costs receive equal, if not better, rates of return than people who buy assets in actively-managed funds with high-maintenance costs.

If you agree, I suggest you start reading some of the many books on the basics of investment, portfolio management, and the psychology of investment (e.g., Schultheis, 2013; Merriman, 2008; Zweig, 2007; Farrell, 2006; Taleb, 2005; Swedroe, 2003; Bernstein, 2002; Ellis, 2002; Belsky and Gilovich, 1999; Lynch, 1989). For example, one of my favorite authors is Merriman (2008). He writes in a simple language the essence of portfolio design and management. He suggests the classes of assets in what he calls "Your Ideal Portfolio," which is the result of many years of research on the types of funds to buy that emulate an index, such as the S&P 500, and that at the same time minimize the risks.

On the other hand, if you are thinking about buying stocks of individual companies, one of my favorite authors on the subject is Lynch (1989). He outlines a simple strategy to pick stocks. Whatever you do, never get in the market without a clear objective and without knowledge of the principles and the risks. Lastly, never buy stocks based on tips from friends, the media, or financial advertisement. They are usually wrong and may cost you dearly. With these remarks, let us take a crash course on the basic steps to invest in the stock market.

Step 1: State your Objectives

Getting in the market without a clear idea of your goals is like going on a trip without knowing your destination. Decide what it is you wish to accomplish with your investment strategy. Put it in writing and refer to it each time you buy or sell an asset, or when things get tough. Your objectives dictate your actions to accomplish them. Do you wish to save over a life time to assure a financially stable retirement? Do you wish to leave some assets to your heirs? Do you want to save for your children's college? Do you want to accumulate money for a medical or other emergency? Do you want to accumulate funds to buy your dream villa in southern Spain? Also, decide the level of risk you can tolerate. Are you a "conservative" investor? Then a low level of risk should be implied in your selected portfolio –one with a greater allocation to fixed income. In other facets of your life, are you a risk taker? After trying hard at an endeavor, do you take the occasional defeat positively and learn from it? Then, objectives associated with greater risks are on the order –greater allocation to stocks.

Step 2: Save for Investing

Develop the habit of regularly saving for investing. For instance, you will need to deduct a percentage of each pay check you receive. You will need to do this for the rest of your working life. This is an obvious pre-requisite for investing, but one easily overlooked by many people. Most people I know, some working in high paying jobs, save little. In fact, many people spend more than what they make. Some of my friends enjoy six-figure incomes and spend just as much. They are income rich, but equity poor. They go through life with the idea that the wealthy income they enjoy will be there forever. For these reasons, most Americans do not save enough for retirement.

There are two ways to save more. One way is to increase your income, or get a promotion, which is usually difficult and sporadic. The other way is to spend less. When I mention this, the immediate reaction I get is " I cannot save more." Do you have a budget? Have you and your partner sat down to review in writing the list of monthly expenses you have? It is an enlightening experience. You will be able to separate your fixed expenses – mortgage payments, utilities, taxes, insurance– from the optional ones. The latter may be things that you think are necessary, but in fact they may not and they may add to a big portion of the budget if you do not pay attention. Do you shop for the things you need, or for emotional comfort? Do you really need to buy groceries online? Do you really need to have the latest model of a car or a phone? Make a list of which things you really need, which ones you want to keep for enjoyment, and which ones you can eliminate. Eliminating unnecessary expenses is like giving yourself a raise.

Many years ago, I resolved to do my own gardening. As a result, I save about $500 a year, and enjoy many fitness benefits. I park my car two miles from the parking lot and walk to the shuttle bus to the main university campus. Yes, I feel a bit old riding with my students but it is healthy, I avoid the stress of the rush hour, I save about $2,000 a year in transportation costs, and about $500 a year in parking expenses. Rather than eating fast food for lunch at a restaurant, I bring a bag with fruit, nuts, and wholesome snacks. The result is not only great financially, it helps the waistline too. I cook more meals at home, some of them gourmet, and cut on restaurant expenses. I prefer to pay for the repairs my car rather than replace it every three years. I am not suggesting to deprive yourself of some pleasurable things you enjoy, which make life meaningful, but only of the superficial things that add to an important portion of the budget, and prevent you from saving more to achieve your financial goals. If you examine your expenses, I am positive you will find many little items you can do without. Eliminating them will increase your savings.

Another easy way to save is to automatically deduct a percentage of each pay check and electronically send it to your brokerage account. A typical ratio is ten percent, which reminds us of the *diezmo*, a compulsory tax deducted by the church in medieval times. Impose yourself a diezmo, which will help satisfy your financial goals. Once the habit is created you do not have to think about it. Of course, remember your objectives once you get a promotion, and maintain your diezmo –ten percent of your higher income. Again, most people I know increase their expenses after a promotion or an increase in income, instead of increasing their savings –a bigger house, a luxury car. An inspiring author to read about the importance of saving and its role in wealth is Clason (2002).

Step 3: Fund your Brokerage Account

Open a brokerage account with one of the online trading companies and automatically deposit your savings. Research the various opportunities available. In the past I have had accounts with TD Ameritrade, Vanguard, and TIAA-CREF. I have had good experiences with them, but I do not endorse anyone in particular. Online trading revolutionized the way stocks are bought and sold in the exchanges. Individual investors no longer need expensive brokers; online commissions are about ten percent of what brokers used to charge in the 1980s. Browse through the sites of these trading companies; read the reviews, and learn about the trading fees. As part of the benefits, some of these companies will make available several online libraries with financial information, annual reports, and independent analysis of many companies. It is easy to be overwhelmed by the amount of financial information available to aid the investor in a decision to buy, or to sell, a stock. Familiarize yourself with these reports and learn to read some key aspects and interpret the graphs. Investing, like anything worth doing, requires regular time of study and analysis. Once you have your account funded, you are set to start buying assets.

Step 4: Decide on Asset Allocation

What kind of assets and in what proportion will be in your portfolio is in direct relationship to your objectives in Step 1 and your assumed risk level. The higher the risk, the higher the return rate from your portfolio, but also the greater the potential short-term loss. The opposite is also true. For our purposes, I assume that your long-term goal is to save for a stable retirement. I reproduce here some of the ideas that research has proven time and again they work for long-term conservative investors. However, I suggest again that this part should be carefully studied and learned from other books specialized in the basics of investment and portfolio management. I present here a simple example to aid the discussion in this chapter.

A widely accepted concept suggests that a portfolio should be divided into classes with 60 percent devoted to stocks and 40 percent devoted to bonds. This is how pension funds of large U. S. companies have traditionally invested most of their money. This model exhibits strong returns and small risks for the long-term investor. The portion allocated to stocks has a higher rate of return, but higher risks, than the portion allocated to bonds. Also, it is assumed here that, in general, the price of stocks fluctuate in opposite directions to those of bonds. In other words, in a bull market the price of stocks are high, while those of bonds are comparatively low. The opposite seems to be true: In a bear market, the price of stocks are low, while those of bonds are high. The opposite cycles in the price of stocks and bonds occur frequently –although not always–, and reduce the risks of the whole portfolio. A low risk, as measured by the price standard deviation, combined with and overall attractive return make the 60/40 percent allocation a popular one.

Many analyst suggest that the actual proportion allocated to stocks and bonds should be a function of other variables, including the age of the investor. The younger the investor the higher the allocation to stocks should be; some suggest a 70/30 ratio for the young investor in his or her twenties. As the investor approaches retirement the ratio devoted to stocks should be decreased. Some suggest that after retirement the proportion should be 50/50. These are suggestions, widely contested among analysts.

Having decided the ratio between stocks and bonds, the next widely accepted premise is that within each class the investor should seek *diversification*. For example, as part of the 40 percent fixed-income portion, one should include intermediate-term government bonds, short-term government bonds, and U. S. Treasury inflation-protected securities (TIPS). Similarly, as part of the 60 percent equity, your portfolio should include large-capitalization *growth* companies; small-capitalization growth companies; large-capitalization *value* companies that are out of favor; small-capitalization value companies; real estate companies; large capitalization international companies head-quartered outside the U. S.; small-capitalization foreign companies; and foreign companies in emerging economies. It has been shown that there are different pricing cycles amongst the various types of companies, sometimes with opposite peaks and lows, which in turn increase the returns of the whole portfolio while reducing the risks. For instance, the timing of recessions in the United States and those in foreign countries sometimes have a substantial lag. Thus, owning assets of both U. S. and foreign companies make a portfolio more stable over time.

If you feel apprehensive about buying stocks of individual companies, especially foreign companies in distant unknown markets, today's investor has at his/her disposal the opportunity to buy stocks of index funds, or stocks of Exchange Trading Funds (ETFs). These are funds that specialize in trading companies that follow a specific index, such as the S&P 500, which is made of large U. S. Companies. For instance, there are some ETFs that buy stocks of companies classified as foreign emerging markets. Alternatively, if one wishes to invest in real estate companies, one may buy stocks in a Real Estate Investment Trust (REIT). These are ETFs that own companies that specialize in trading in real estate investments –housing, buildings, shopping malls. Some of these funds may possess hundreds of companies in the same category. Alternatively, you can buy stocks of an ETF fund that specializes in short-term government bonds. Some of the stocks owned by the fund have different risks levels and different price fluctuations, but the overall value of such ETF stock has a significant lower risk than that of an individual company in the same category. Unlike mutual funds, which are actively managed, have high maintenance costs, and have limited liquidity because of restrictive ownership times, many ETFs are passively managed, have low maintenance costs, and have immediate liquidity like that of any stock.

As stated, the focus of this book is on intermediate to long-term investing. This absolutely excludes investment products designed for the short-term investor. For example, you will find highly speculative ETFs labeled as Ultra, 3X, Double Long, Inverse, or Commodity. They advertise unbelievably high returns, but beware they are associated with high risks, especially for investors who keep them longer than one day. Read the experts' reports before you invest in them (e.g., Justice, 2009).

I refer the reader to more authoritative treatises on how to select index funds or ETFs. For instance, Merriman (2008) has excellent ideas about what specific funds to buy and in what proportions. Table 4.1 shows an example of a typical portfolio composed exclusively of ETFs. It depicts a tentative distribution among the different classes of assets. It also includes in the third column the ticker symbols of some ETF funds in each category. This is an example of a tentative portfolio. A suggestion to stimulate further study. I remark that I do not endorse any particular fund, nor do I receive any incentive or commission from any of them. Before you invest in any of these funds, or any other fund, you should do your homework. Your brokerage account provides access to an online library with the reports and profiles of each of these funds and many more. Study in detail the description of the fund; see how the price has performed in the past in relation to the underlying index, in relation to other market indices, or in relation to similar funds; note what are the risks as stated by independent analysts –usually available on the same page of the report–, and compare them to your objectives; study the tables that describe the past returns or losses for each dollar invested; and examine the list of companies the fund owns.

Table 4.1: A Portfolio Example Composed of ETFs

	ASSET CLASS	EXAMPLES
	U. S. Large Cap Growth (8 %)	VUG, VOT, MGK, IWP
	U. S. Small Cap Growth (8 %)	VBK, VTWG
	U. S. Large Cap Value (8 %)	VYM, VTV, VOE
	U. S. Small Cap Value (8 %)	IJS, VBR
STOCKS (60 %)	U. S. REIT, (7 %)	VNQ, RWR
	Foreign Large Cap (7 %)	VEU, VT, VEA, VXUS, VGK, EFG, ACWV, VNQI
	Foreign Small Cap (7 %)	VSS, SCZ, SCHC
	Foreign Emerging Markets (7 %)	VWO, EEMV, SCHE
	Int. Term Gov. Funds. (12 %)	BIV, VGIT, BND, AGG
BONDS (40 %)	Short Term Gov. Funds (15 %)	VGSH, SCHO
	TIPS (13 %)	TIP

Now, it is possible that you may be inclined to take higher risks, with the possibility of higher returns, by investing in stocks of individual companies, instead of or in addition to ETFs and index funds. Here again, you need a detailed study of potential companies. In order to select a company to invest, begin by picking between ten and fifteen companies from the same industry, all with good financial records. This involves viewing each company report online for the previous years. The amount of information available is overwhelming. In particular, look for a consistent increase in gross revenue over the years; a consistent growth in net profits over time; pay attention to the proportion of long-term debt relative to its capital; see that the balance sheet has a solid stockholder equity; and make sure that after short-term lows and highs, the price of the company shares exhibits a consistent increase over time. Also, read about the plans management has for the future. Look for a good management plan or a company's rationale for product development and growth. As you can see, this is simple old fashioned common sense. However, you will find in the reports and analyses a myriad of index measures, complicated financial language, and opinions sometimes widely divergent amongst the advisors. In the end, one should look for a simple assurance that the company is financially stable and with a future in its industry. As my father used to say, "So much financial jargon! At the end of the day, is this company making any money?"

Having decided on a portfolio allocation, and having completed your own financial analysis of each finalist in a set of companies, ETFs or index funds, you now have a good idea about which funds might be suitable to buy. You have completed the *rational analysis* of the process. I would suggest at this point to proceed with the *irrational or intuitive* part of your analysis before you make a decision. This is because, as we have discussed, much of the buying and selling trends in the market are only in part the result of logical and conscientious analysis of the financials of a company. Many investors buy motivated by greed, or sell subject to fear. Being aware of emotional motivations in the market may help you take advantage of, or avoid, certain trends.

Your illogical mind, your unconscious emotional self, has the possibility to access latent aspirations and wishes you may be unaware of at a conscious level. In addition, if you make the collected financial information available to your unconscious mind, it will analyze it in intuitive and creative ways you could not possibly foresee. Lastly, if we adhere to psychological theory that suggests the individual unconscious has access to a collective unconscious, then we have in principle the possibility to perceive the collective public emotions as they relate to the stock market. Correctly interpreting these might be crucial at the time of deciding to buy, or to sell, assets. Most people are completely unaware of their different levels of the psyche, let alone how to access and use them. They are so absorbed in the daily stresses and routines of existence, that they forget there is a greater picture of life.

I am not suggesting you would go an make an important financial decision on a haunch. On the contrary, I insist that *first* you do the financial study of the company as described above, and *second* you make it available to deeper levels of the self. There are several levels in our mind, each with specific abilities, which we may employ for our benefit. Normally, we are only aware of and trust our rational mind with its logical and inductive features. We also have an unconscious mind with rarely-used intuitive and other latent abilities. In addition, there are deeper levels of the mind with higher forms of thinking. You can access the intuitive wisdom of your unconscious by means of meditation exercises. There are simple ways to do this, but they require time and patience. In my book "The Three Spirits" (Serrano, 2011), I transmitted and reinterpreted the wisdom of ancient civilizations, which not only knew about the unconscious –rediscovered by Freud in the 20th century–, but they also knew how to use it for applications. I explain in detail how to access and take advantage of other parts of our mind. I present specific examples and practical step-by-step exercises to improve your life, solve problems, including picking stocks. Knowing onself, and exploring and solving our negative emotions, is a rewarding experience in and of itself, not just to make money. If you follow this path of self discovery and growth, there are greater rewards, including a happy and harmonious existence with yourself and others.

As I stated before, you should not believe anything an analyst or an "expert" suggests until you have done your own study and verify that it is correct. Likewise, please do not believe anything I just said concerning the unconscious. I invite you to explore the possibility that there is a helping hand, a friend if you will, within yourself. I encourage you to read more about the topic, try some meditation exercises, record your experiences, and only believe that which you have proven to be truthful. You will find unexpected new ideas, but also you will discover your unconscious disagrees with many of your past and current decisions and activities, and that is why it sabotaged some of your plans. To succeed at any endeavor, you need the agreement and cooperation of all parts of yourself. Pay attention and you will find a more satisfying life ahead of you.

Investing requires time, concentration, and self discipline. In the end, you will have decided on a portfolio distribution and the assets to buy. It is time to act, that is to purchase a number of shares (e.g., one hundred) from each of the assets in your portfolio to match the allocation proportions. As you continue to fund your online account, you can automatically direct these funds to buy assets in the prescribed proportions. What we have said about after tax accounts is also valid for pretax accounts. If you have an employer-based IRA, you should start to actively manage it by following the steps outlined above. In other words, decide on a portfolio allocation and select the best companies or funds in which to invest. Perhaps you will apply the same asset allocation to your IRA and after tax brokerage accounts, perhaps not. My point is: take the reins of managing your IRA account. Do not do what most employees do, which is neglect it for many years until they approach retirement, only to find that they could have maximized returns and reduce the costs significantly.

Step 5: Limit your Expenses and Tax Liability
Expenses and taxes can significantly reduce your returns if you do not pay attention. Try to actively identify them, reduce them, or when possible completely eliminate them. One big expense is the fee financial planners charge for their services. A one percent in annual expenses seems innocuous enough, but by some estimates you would reduce the ending account balance by a whopping seventeen percent over twenty

years. There is an easy way to avoid it: Do not pay for investment services; do your homework and learn to invest on your own. Brokerage houses may also charge an annual maintenance fee to accounts with less than a certain balance amount. Then, choose a house that does not impose those fees.

Trading costs is an expense an investor pays when buying or selling stocks, bonds, and other securities. Some online trading companies charge a flat fee each time you buy or sell. Thus, an easy way to limit your expenses is to limit the number of times you trade a stock. This should be easy if you adhere to your long-term financial objectives. For example, rebalance your portfolio once a year only. Some trading companies have a list of funds you can buy or sell without a fee, provided you hold on to the shares a minimum of time (e.g., one month). This is to prevent day trading, which drives expenses up for stock holders. The list of these commission-free companies may include attractive funds with solid financial records, high investment returns, and at the same time with low annual expenses (e.g., notably the Vanguard family of funds). Investigate them.

Now, mutual funds trading costs are usually not explicitly disclosed. Some have a high-turnover, suggesting the fund managers seem more interested in maximizing their commissions, instead of minimizing your costs. Hence, buy low-turnover index funds. Also, funds charge investors for administration and management. These are recurring expenses you can easily identify. Each fund must disclose what it charges investors annually. Look for it in the fund's profile. Select funds that charge 0.20 percent or less per year. Remember to look for similar hidden fees and expenses when selecting an employer-based IRA plan.

There are two classes of mutual funds: *load* funds, which charge a sales commission up front when you invest in them, and no load funds, which do not have a commission. Seek and buy exclusively in no load funds. The commissions charged by load funds are such that they cloud any higher returns they may have relative to no load funds.

When selecting funds, check the annual tax loss ratio, which combined with annual expense charges may add to a significant loss over the years. The subject of investment taxes is complex; I refer the reader to the many books on it. One simple thing every one should do is to keep good records of purchases, sales, and capital gains distributions. Knowing and adjusting the cost basis of any transaction will help you detect errors, particularly if you reinvested some of the profits on the same fund. Also, when selling stocks, try to balance as much as possible the sale of profitable stocks with those of unprofitable ones. That will reduce your taxes. In a bad year, the losses from the sales of securities will help reduce your taxable income up to a maximum allowable amount. The excess loss can be deferred to future tax years. Read the instructions of the Individual Tax Return, From 1040, Schedule D –where you report capital gains. Some writers advise to keep the tax-efficient funds in after tax accounts, and to leave the tax-inefficient funds to tax-sheltered IRA accounts. Learn about the tax advantages and rules regarding IRAs and Roth IRAs.

Step 6: Manage your Portfolio

Now that you have an automatic savings plan in action and a well-researched portfolio with assets in the market, it is time to regularly adjust them to conform to your objectives. The value of the assets in your portfolio change according to the continuous fluctuations in the stock market. As said before, you should disregard the daily or weekly fluctuations in stock prices.

However, during a bull market the equity portion of assets will increase faster in price than those of the fixed-income portion. Likewise, during a bear market, the equity portion will decrease in price faster than the fixed-income assets. This discrepancies make the portfolio gradually depart form the prescribed proportions. For example, if your portfolio prescribes a 60 percent in stocks and a 40 percent in bonds, during a bull market stock appreciation will cause the proportion of stocks to rise to 65 percent, while the proportion of bonds decrease to 35 percent. In order to keep the portfolio on target, you should sell some shares in one or more of the assets in the exceeding category and transfer them to those in the receding category. This is called portfolio *rebalance*. When you rebalance the portfolio, you adjust the proportion of assets to keep them aligned with your long-term objectives.

At the same time, preparing to rebalance a portfolio constitutes a good opportunity to assess the performance of each asset. Reading the company reports, you decide if the returns are according to the initial expectations. Thus, rebalancing also includes eliminating certain assets that under perform, keeping the good ones, and acquiring new ones if necessary.

When rebalancing a portfolio, you sell assets that have increased in price, collect your profits, and invest them in securities that have decreased in value. That is exactly the correct strategy: sell expensive assets, and buy inexpensive ones. When the tables turn, in the next rebalance you sell the ones you bought at low cost –now turn expensive– and buy the ones you sold expensively –now turn cheap. It sounds simple enough, buy cheap and sell expensive. However, that is not what most people do: They buy expensive assets that have performed well during a bull, perhaps following a tip from friends or the media. They think they will miss out on the great returns that they believe will continue to increase indefinitely. On the other hand, during a bear market they sell depressed assets that have declined in value. They act out of fear that they will lose everything if they do not act quickly and salvage something. This is the cycle of greed and fear that deprives investors of their rational thinking and overcomes them with negative emotions. The result is the loss of financial assets and the defeat of long-term goals. The solution is to act with discipline, while opposing the negative emotions of the prevailing market conditions.

Besides exercising the correct attitude, the timing of rebalancing should be planned, in principle. Too frequent rebalancing is counter productive and may in fact defeat your objectives. First, remember that selling profitable assets generate a tax liability. Second, frequent buying or selling generates trading expenses. Lastly, and more importantly, you may be eliminating assets that seem out of sync with your objectives, but if you wait a little longer, they may reveal themselves as suitable. Likewise, you may be acquiring assets that seem over performing, but a longer observation may reveal them unsuitable to your objectives. Examine your feelings and decide wether you are buying out of greed, or because you studied the company and found it suitable to your objectives. Similarly, when things look grim explore your feelings and decide wether you are selling out of fear, or because the asset has performed well and you are collecting a profit.

From above, the timing of rebalance should be planned. The question is, when should one rebalance a portfolio? Some authors argue this should be done a maximum of once a year at the same time of the year, regardless of how the market is doing. This comes after the conclusion by many that the market cannot be defeated on a permanent basis. In other words, it is difficult to constantly buy on the cheap and sell on the expensive so that a profit is always assured. This is also a good advice for people who are prone to the greed-fear cycle. An unconscious regular rebalance has been shown to produce good returns, while minimizing risks.

The above strategy underlines the assumption that markets are completely unpredictable and that market cycles do not exist. Granted, we cannot predict the actual value of the DJIA on a given day. However, in Chapter 3 we learned that we can predict the cycles of the market in a broad statistical sense. The research I reported suggests there are in fact astronomical cycles that exhibit a correlation, under certain conditions, to market cycles. We learned about these cycles, and cultivated the right mental attitude and discipline. Can we plan and prepare for a portfolio adjustment and rebalance without significantly increasing our risks? I think we can.

Rebalancing Under the Jupiter-Saturn Cycle

In Chapter 3, we examined in detail historical events in the stock market and its relationship to the Jupiter-Saturn Market Growth Potential (MGP). Let us now look at a complete MGP cycle of about twenty years.

Figure 4.1 shows the last complete MGP cycle (1995-2015). Remember that the left scale measures the MGP from 0 to 180 degrees, and the right scale measures the DJIA. The MGP cycle resembles a sine wave starting at 90 degrees –when Jupiter is in *quadrature* with Saturn–, it reaches a peak at 180 degrees –when Jupiter is in conjunction with Saturn–, then returns to a value of 90 degrees. This completes the first half of the cycle. The second half is opposite but symmetrical to the first. In other words, the MGP decreases from 90 to a minimum of 0 degrees –when Jupiter is in opposition to Saturn–, then gradually rises to 90 degrees –when Jupiter is again in quadrature with Saturn. This completes a cycle of 19.87 years in duration.

On the other hand, the DJIA has a cycle of growing and receding parts which are not symmetric about the peak. It resembles a kinematic flood wave in a river, with a sharp front end and a long back tail. The rising period usually lasts much longer than the receding period, which is often of relatively short duration and characterized by sharp falls. Over a long period, the magnitude of the DJIA significantly overcomes and exceeds any drops. After studying 120 years of market data, I can state a fundamental principle of the stock market:

Over a long time, the natural state of the stock market is to slowly grow, unless it is temporarily perturbed by intervals of quick losses.

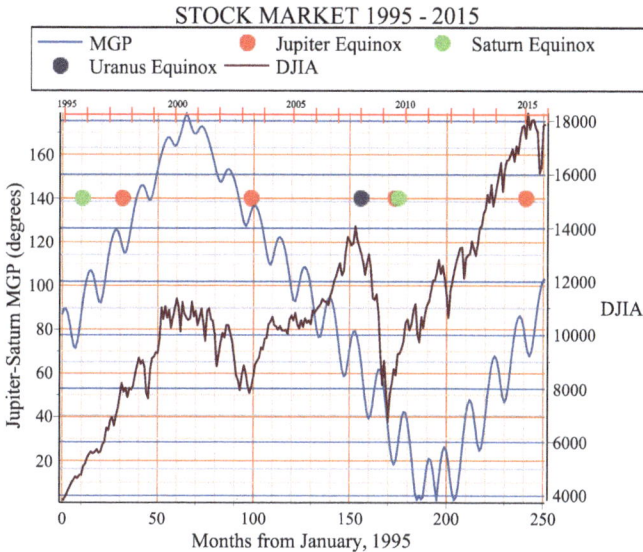

Figure 4.1: The last complete cycle of the Jupiter-Saturn MGP

There is nothing new about this. In the past, many analysts have stated the same idea in many ways, while encouraging investors to look at the big picture, instead of the short-term aspects. This suggests we should look closely at the relatively long periods of growth and see if we can used them to our advantage, or at least avoid the short-term drops. Let us see how we can apply this principle along with the MGP.

I indicated that the value of the MGP at a given time is not as important as its rising or lowering trend. Thus, in general, a rising MGP indicates a potential for a bull market, whereas a decreasing MGP indicates a potential for a bear market. However, I found that a rising MGP has a better relationship and affinity with a rising DJIA, whereas a decreasing MGP does not always correlate well with a decreasing DJIA. While the MGP is decreasing, the DJIA may temporarily contradict it and actually increase, and the affect of a decreasing MGP may abruptly manifest at the end of the cycle. I also found that planetary equinoxes sometimes have a disruptive effect on the MGP cycle.

From Figure 4.1, I should add another interesting feature. The intermediate point of the cycle, that is when the MGP is 90 degrees, appears to be associated with times of relative calm in the market (i.e., no sharp jumps in value), *provided there are no planetary equinoxes in the vicinity*. I went back and double checked this with 120 years of historical data. During the period 1900-2020, when the MGP was about 90 degrees there was relative calm in the market. Since 1900 the MGP has crossed this value almost fifteen times. It remains to see if this is a representative number confirming a trend. Nevertheless, the best we can hope for is that the characteristics of a historical records will repeat themselves in the future. I should remark at this point that in this particular aspect my results disagree with accepted facts in *astrology* (as opposed to astronomy). Astrological predictions affirm that quadratures (i.e., the times when the MGP is 90 degrees) are negative for the market. My result suggests that, at least for Jupiter and Saturn, quadratures are neutral.

Let us imagine for a moment we have the power to travel in time back to 1995 and decided to rebalance our portfolio during the neutral times when the MGP was near 90 degrees. How did our portfolio perform? Looking again at Figure 4.1, we can appreciate that the first rebalance would have occurred at the beginning of 1995. We could say that by doing so we would have missed the bull market of 1995-1999 and lost the opportunity to make *more* money. However, with the second rebalance towards the end of 2005, we also missed the agony of the bear market of 2000-2003, but on the other hand we collected the profits of the short bull market of 2003-2005. In addition, between 1995 and 2005 the DJIA rose from about 4,000 to about 11,000, reflecting an outstanding profit, while significantly saving in trading expenses.

Let us continue our imaginary example above. Returning to Figure 4.1, the next time to rebalance would have been towards the middle of or late 2015. I would have been cautious about it after seeing an ensuing Jupiter equinox and its potential effects. Let us say we ignored this and we went ahead with rebalancing. We can see that since the previous rebalance in 2005 and the current one in 2015, the DJIA rose from about 11,000 to about 18,000. This remarkable increase, with its associated returns to the average portfolio is further enhanced by the fact that we would have missed the Great Recession of 2007-2009. By staying out of the market all together, and not participating in the mass panic, we had avoided many losses. Once again, this is admittedly difficult to do, but it makes sense for the long-term investor.

Therefore, if we emphasize the long-term performance of a portfolio, it makes sense to delay rebalancing, and perhaps to limit it to times when the MGP is about 90 degrees. If we look at the larger picture –a fundamental principle in this book–, rather than being obsessively worried about the short-term details, we will benefit enormously, while substantially reducing the risks. If we look exclusively at the act of rebalancing among existing holdings, once every ten years seems beneficial. This of course excludes regular portfolio analysis to eliminate or expand holdings, which should be done frequently. I realize what I am proposing goes against common wisdom in portfolio management, but the numbers support my premise.

The greatest obstacle to the foregoing is not financial; it is psychological. The bear market of 2000-2003, with the collapse of the dot-com companies, brought substantial losses to many. The investor who adhered to his/her long-term objectives stayed out of the market all together, firmly believing the market will recover eventually, as it did, while rejecting the internal fears of total loss. The investor with a well-diversified portfolio recovered. The investor who did not own stocks in dot-com companies fully recovered. Most technology startups at that time were financially crippled; some did not report any profits at all. Thus, any conscientious investor who studied their financials (Step 4 in the last section) would have rejected the idea of investing in them anyway.

Maximizing Returns with the MGP

In the last section, I proposed a strategy consisting of scheduling each portfolio rebalance around the times when the MGP is near 90 degrees, provided there are no planetary equinoxes within a few months before or after this event. I believe this is a sensible strategy for the long-term investor with a well-diversified portfolio seeking the returns of a typical market index, while minimizing the risks.

Now that we know the existence of astronomical cycles that may influence the market, the question arises, can we use them to maximize returns? Trading beyond the neutral points of the MGP may increase returns, but significantly increase the risks. If you are a conservative long-term investor you would *not* follow the suggestions I give below. However, if your tolerance for risk is higher, perhaps you may try them. Then, there is also the investor who is conservative with *most* of his/her assets as described before, but who wishes to speculate with *a small portion* of funds. I have been one of them.

Throughout most of my investment life, I have been a conservative investor with most of my assets. I was thinking about an early retirement and I never risked defeating that goal or the financial safety of the family for the sake of an elusive short-term gain. However, there have been times when I risked a portion of extra cash, which never amounted to more than five percent of my net worth, for the purpose of achieving a higher return. Destined for speculation, this cash was put to use at times when I thought I could beat the market. In my mind, I accepted the possibility that I could lose it all if my experiment went wrong. Once again, there is nothing secret about the strategy, except for the timing to make your move:

Step 1: Plan which Assets to Trade
This is no different from Step 4 in the portfolio planning section before. Study at length company profiles, reports, and past performance. Avoid new startups that promise great returns, but do not offer any

documented evidence of past performance. Carefully select which stocks you will buy well ahead of time. Never invest on a haunch, a tip, or an impulse before studying a stock. As stated before, you can use your intuition *after* you do your homework and provide your unconscious self with a logical financial analysis. Make a list of these companies with good financials in an industry you like, with the intention of buying their shares when the time is right. By limiting the list to businesses with good financials, you are minimizing the risk of losing everything in an eventual corporate bankruptcy. In addition, if you bought at the wrong time, and the stock keeps losing value, the probability of a good company to recover is greater than one with poor financials. Remember, you do not lose anything if you wait and do not sell. Having a list of your favorite companies, you patiently wait until the market drops. This may take months, perhaps years.

Step 2: When the MGP Declines, Buy After the Market Drops

Here you wait until there is a significant decline in the market, not for a period of a few days, but months. Observe the trends in the MGP. When it is declining, there is a potential for the market to drop. In addition, look for equinoxes, those astronomical events that we learned to fear and to avoid, now they are our friends, a source of opportunity. Let us see an example from historical records. Imagine you traveled into the past and bought depressed stocks of good companies. In Step 2, timing is very important. When should you have bought them? Looking again at Figure 4.1 for market drops in the last twenty years, you would have made your move to buy some shares in your list of companies around April 2003. You would have waited patiently until the effects of the declining MGP and those of the Jupiter equinox manifested in the market. The key word here is *after* the market has dropped substantially. There is a judgement call here, of course. If you make your move and the market keeps dropping, relax. Remember, you bought a good stock. In all likelihood, it will recover.

In any case, before you actually buy a stock in your list, spend a few minutes reviewing the latest company report to see if it still looks attractive, and of course see if the price of the stock has substantially decreased along with the market. Otherwise, it does not make any sense buying it.

A second opportunity to buy would have occurred in the middle of 2009. The MGP was close to zero, combined with the effects of the Jupiter, Saturn, and Uranus equinoxes. The market lost over 40 percent in a few months, but it was then beginning to recover. Once again, one should wait until a noticeable downward effect has occurred.

Step 3: Sell when the MGP is Rising and Near its Peak

The last step is to wait until the MGP is approaching its climax. When the MGP reaches 180 degrees, Jupiter is in conjunction with Saturn, and the potential for market growth is maximum. At the same time, the forces that tend to destabilize the market begin to take effect. Make your move to sell the shares of the companies you bought in Step 2 when the MGP is approaching 180 degrees, but well before it occurs. As you wait for the peak of the MGP, you risk losing the opportunity to sell; if you miss it, you will have to wait for a while, perhaps years, before the next opportunity comes.

I recommend selling when the MGP reaches 120 degrees, not later. Once again, do not let greed make you miss the opportunity. I heard it before: "If I wait a little longer, my profits will be greater." I have also heard the complaint of a friend who cautiously sold in time, only to find the market kept rising afterwards: "Oh, if I had just waited a little longer!" My answer in both cases is the same: It is better to sell in time and collect some profits, than to wait too long and risk losing the opportunity. When the market drops, it does it in a fast and precipitous way. Then, it is too late to sell.

If you were successful at the end of this step, you will have collected extra profits you may now use to reinvest in the standard portfolio, or to keep in a money market fund waiting for the next opportunity to buy (Step 2) in the next cycle. As you can see, the strategy is simple. It requires studying the companies to invest, planning your moves carefully, and patiently waiting for the right time to act. At the same time, you attentively watch the evolution of the MGP, the occurrence of other astronomical phenomena (e.g., equinoxes), the magnitude of the DJIA and other market indexes. Also, you must read the economic analyses and the political developments around the globe. They may give clues about other events that may affect the market. Pay attention, observe your surroundings, and plan with confidence the attainment of your goals with the knowledge that astronomical cycles will help, if you work with them, instead of against them. My grandfather use to say "Most people are half asleep; those who are awake are in a state of constant amazement." Lastly, and above all, enjoy your journey; see what you can learn from the occasional and inevitable setback, and try again.

Overcoming Psychological Barriers, the Biggest Obstacle to Successful Investing

I include a short discussion on a topic taken for granted, but often disregarded by many investors. The most important obstacles to achieving financial objectives with the stock market are psychological. They manifest in a number of ways. First, it is the reluctance to save for investment. We live in a culture where living for the moment, and enjoying immediate gratification rules the mentality of many. Spending extra money now that we can, instead of saving some for an uncertain future, makes intuitive sense. This goes in concert with our obsessive preoccupation for the details of everyday live, instead of focusing on the bigger picture, the greater purpose of things. The same could be said about the reluctance of many people to open an IRA account. Their employers usually match, sometimes double, the employee's contribution, and any capital gains will be tax deferred until the user retires. It does make good financial sense, and yet many employees fail to act.

The solution is discipline and concentration. Pay attention to the advice of philosophers and inspirational writers. The bigger picture is what ultimately brings lasting rewards. Delaying gratification fosters growth, character, and ultimately profound satisfaction. I hear some of my university students saying, "I don't have money to save; I only make $12.00 an hour." In truth, even with a small hourly wage, she could save $1.20 an hour (i.e., 10%). Remember the power of compound interest. Over a long period of time –and time is what young investors have–, a small regular contribution becomes a sizable capital. I am not advocating a monastic life. On the contrary, give yourself some small reward you want each time you get paid, but also remember your long-term goals and maintain a constant proportion of savings regardless of how much you make.

The second psychological obstacle manifests as neglect to spend the required regular time to study and plan investments. It has many justifications, including "I'm too busy; I don't have time for that." What could be more important than planning and executing the means to attain your dreams? The solution again is discipline and concentration. Resolve to spend a few minutes a week, or an hour per month, to plan and review your portfolio. If you constantly remember your goals and dreams, you might actually enjoy it.

The third kind of psychological obstacle occurs when an investor is executing a carefully-planned rebalance, or a well-thought strategic sale during a bull market. Sometimes presents itself as criticism from friends: "Why are you selling such a great stock? Everyone is buying it. You will lose a lot of money." It also appears with more force just before a strategic buy during or after a bear market. This comes as a subtle hunch from your fearful unconscious: "Why are you buying stocks that have lost so much value? You are crazy; everyone is selling; you will be ruined." Selling what everyone is buying or buying what everyone is selling makes us doubt. Is it possible that I am wrong? How can it be that everyone is wrong and I am right? These are emotional feelings every investor faces sooner or later, even if what you are doing is the result of rational thinking and careful planning.

The solution lies in remembering your long-term plans, believing in yourself, trusting the careful study that concluded with the decision to act now. You have done your homework in applying the basic principles of investing. You also remember what you learned in this book about the behavior of the stock market for the past 120 years. The possibility of being wrong has a low probability. The most you can lose is time, and over time eventual losses will be recovered.

The fourth and most important class of psychological obstacles to achieve financial goals is much more serious than neglect to save, laziness to study and plan, or doubt at the threshold of an action, described above. This obstacle has potentially disastrous consequences. It manifests in two extremes, avarice and panic. The former incites the investor to buy, when s/he should sell or do nothing. The latter urges the investor to sell, when s/he should buy or do nothing. Both extremes manifest with little or no rational thinking, and mostly out of emotional impulsiveness. Every investor, sooner or later, will be tested with these blockages; whether you pass or fail will determine your success or failure as a long-term investor.

Let us examine one of the extremes. A perfect example is the current market conditions. Since the last great recession, the DJIA has tripled, an unprecedented event in the history of the market. Let us disregard for the moment the many reasons analysts give for this phenomenon. Some may be correct; it does not matter. The point is that investors worldwide continue to buy and to drive the DJIA up and up. This despite the best financial logic and rational thinking. Most stocks are overvalued; the Price/Earnings ratio has skyrocketed for most stocks. It does not make any financial sense to buy stocks now; on the contrary it makes sense to sell and collect profits. Yet, people continue to buy. They believe that this unprecedented bull market will last forever. They have this irresistible urge to buy stocks of companies that have rallied in value –some with poor financials–, and that they are going to lose the greatest opportunity of their lives if they do not buy now, because these assets will continue to increase forever. This greed, this insatiable desire to accumulate more future profits, rather than collect a smaller but sensible amount now, defeats any long-term financial plans. At the very least, the investor is buying a very expensive stock. The same investor who falls pray of greed is prone to succumb to panic as soon as the market drops, and this takes us to the other extreme.

Let us remember the Great Recession of 2007-2009. From 2003 to about September 2007, the market was rallying and enjoying investor exuberance, not unlike the one now. Then came October 2007. When the stock market drops, and it happens sooner or later, it does so in a swift and turbulent way. Then, the fear of total loss suddenly experienced by some investors is amplified and propagated fast to the masses. Soon everyone rushes to sell. They fear that if they do not sell immediately, the stock will keep dropping and they will lose everything. They feel it is better to sell at any price and avoid a total loss. The mass sellout actually accelerates the rate of decline in the price of assets.

The fear of market collapse is exacerbated by many negative mental statements one receives at this time. They include "There is going to be a worldwide depression;" "the market and the economy will never recover;" "This is the end of the world order and the institutions as we knew them;" "I will lose everything I saved in my life."

Of course, these fatalist statements are completely irrational. From what we have learned form the analysis of historical data, the market always recovers. Yes, it may take some time, perhaps years, but eventually it does. Hence, the first line of defense against these feelings is to look at the historical evidence and to offer your unconscious fears some reassurances from the logic of your careful planning over the years, while reminding it that the occasional drop in the market was to be expected; you knew about it and you prepared for it.

While counteracting irrational fear with logic, during this time the second line of defense is to get out of the market all together, unless you are preparing for a strategic buyout, as I described in the last section. During the market drops of 1987, 2001, and 2007, I remember entertaining some of the fears and doubts described above, while considering to abandon my plans and join the hysterical sellout. One of the things that helped me was a firm decision to stay out of the market completely until after it stabilized. I did not do anything to my portfolio; I did not even check the numbers or the news; I remember not logging into my accounts for months. Having done your investment homework, if you do not have the stomach to endure a drop, the best thing at this time is *to do nothing*.

I believe panic during a market drop is the greatest obstacle to successful investing. Yielding to panic, and selling at a very low price, is the greatest mistake one can make. Some of my friends lost hundreds of thousands of their hard-earned retirement savings during market drops. Some of my readers may be arguing now, and rightfully so, that extreme negative emotions are not easily controlled with logic. Emotions, good or bad, come from the lower self or the unconscious mind. Some of them erupt at times with such power that it is not possible to suppress them with just positive thinking. They overpower us at times of anger, rage, or profound sadness, not just fear of loss. They are a source of distress and unhappiness, not just an obstacle to sensible investment decisions. Eliminating negative emotions opens a path to self growth, harmony within ourselves and with others, happiness, and of course successful investing. To overcome these bursts, you have to find the source of these emotions, perhaps originated in the distant pass, and eliminate the energy associated with them.

I am not suggesting to hire a psychologist to deal with the stock market anxiety. It is an expensive and lengthy proposition. Besides, most traditional talk therapies fail to address *the cause* of negative emotions; the best they can do is to help you manage your distress. Certainly, for deep complex trauma, phobias, and serious fixations that interfere with job and family, traditional therapy with a professional is the only way to go. However, for most mild negative emotions, there are new alternatives everyone can try.

How does one eliminate negative emotions, fears of loss, and panic during a market drop? There are new self-help energy therapy techniques, such as *Thought Field Therapy* (TFT) and *Emotional Freedom Technique* (EFT). These are new techniques that make use of the energy meridians in the body. They are similar to acupuncture, but without needles, and intended for the emotions. The stimulation of the body-end meridian points has been shown to discharge the trapped energy associated intense fear and eliminate a negative emotion. When confronted by the urge to sell everything during a market drop, all you need to do is to sit for a few minutes and follow a precise protocol that stimulates some points in your face, breasts, and arms with your fingers, while concentrating on the fear. These constitute permanent cures. For a short introduction, please see Serrano (2011). More details and illustrations with practical applications can be seen in Salomon (2011). These techniques can also be used to eliminate negative emotions and fixations in general. By working regularly on eliminating our negative emotions, we gradually become calmer, more tolerant, and compassionate; we make less mistakes and project inner harmony that extends to better relationships with others. We stop wasting time with inner conflicts and self contradictions. In essence, we exhibit the attributes of happiness. I encourage you to try them. There is nothing to lose, except some time and your negative emotions, and much to gain, including better investment decisions.

Summary of the Effect of Environmental Astronomy on the Stock Market

This study suggests that astronomical events in the solar system have an intrinsic relationship with the stock market. The events that play an important role include the angular distance between the large outer planets, planetary equinoxes, the distance between the large outer planets and the Sun, and the distance between the large outer planets and the Earth. For applications, the most important findings may be summarized as follows:

1. The Market Growth Potential (MGP) is defined as the supplementary angle between two planets, as observed from the Earth.

2. The Jupiter-Saturn MGP seems to have a direct relationship with the DJIA. As the MGP increases, the DJIA has the potential for a corresponding increase. As the MGP decreases, the DJIA has a potential for a corresponding decrease.

3. The MGP increases for about ten years, and then decreases for about ten years.

4. The MGP has a better affinity to bull markets, when both signals gradually rise, than to bear markets when the DJIA may fall via short-term drops, followed by short-term recoveries.

5. Sometimes, a descending MGP cycle contradicts a rising DJIA, and the diminishing effects of the MGP are only felt towards the end of the cycle.

6. Within a few months prior or after the occurrence of a planet's equinox, there may be sharp declines in the DJIA.

7. Within a few months prior or after the occurrence of a planet's equinox, the effect of a rising MGP may be reversed, and the effect of a declining MGP may be accelerated.

8. An increasing distance between a planet and the Sun, and/or between a planet and the Earth, appears to have a beneficial effect on the DJIA.

9.   A decreasing distance between a planet and the Sun, and/or between a planet and the Earth, appears to have a detrimental effect on the DJIA.

10.   Planetary distances, equinoxes, and the MGP interact in a complex manner.

11.   For practical applications, all astronomical events can be predicted accurately in the future.

Market Conditions in the Near Future, 2019-2025

It is now time to extend the mathematical simulations to forecast the astronomical conditions in the near future, and make inferences about the possible implications for the stock market. Figure 4.2 shows the evolution of the Jupiter-Saturn MGP with time for the period 2019-2025. For the year 2019, it shows the dramatic increase in the DJIA from about 22,700 in January to almost 28,000 in December 2019. In agreement with this, the MGP rises from about 150 degrees in January 2019 to about 162 degrees in December.

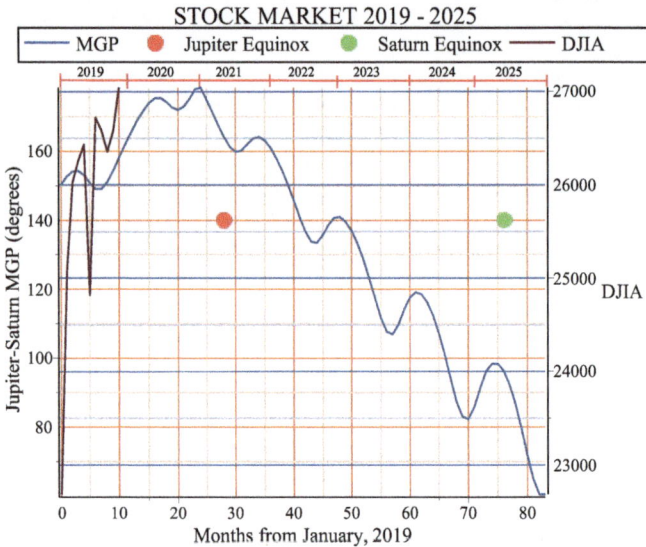

Figure 4.2: The Jupiter-Saturn MGP, 2019-2025

The small ups and downs in the MGP are the result of corrections due to the Earth's orbit around the Sun. Continuing the trend of the past few years, the MGP will continue to rise to its peak of 180 degrees by December, 2020, but most of 2020 will experience a MGP of over 170 degrees. Beginning January 2021, the MGP will begin the next descending cycle to about 62 degrees by December 2025, and will continue descending beyond that.

Potentially, the DJIA is expected to continue increasing in value at least to the first quarter of 2020, in agreement with the increasing MGP. However, Figure 4.2 also shows the occurrence of the next Jupiter equinox in May 2021. We have learned from past experience that the occurrence of a Jupiter equinox may disrupt a rising MGP, or accelerate the decline of a descending MGP for a period of a few months before and after the date of the equinox. According to this, it is possible the DJIA may begin to experience periods of rapid decline in 2020 and beyond. It remains to be seen wether or not the astronomical conditions prevail, or are overridden by other social, economical, or political conditions. Figure 4.2 also shows the MGP will reach 90 degrees in the middle of 2024, which in the past coincided with periods of market neutrality propitious for portfolio rebalance. However, one must be careful with the approaching of a Saturn equinox in May 2025, which may promote periods of market turbulence (i.e., it may enhance a declining MGP).

From historical records, we learned that the distance of Jupiter from the Sun may be a mitigating, or an enhancing variable. For instance, I noted in Figure 3.3 (Chapter 3), that during the current bull market of 2010-2020 an increasing MGP may have been enhanced by an increasing distance of Jupiter from the Sun. Also in Figure 3.6, I remarked that during the Great Recession of 2007-2009 the effect of a decreasing MGP may have been exacerbated by a decreasing distance of Jupiter to the Sun. However, I did not find this effect in all of the historical events examined.

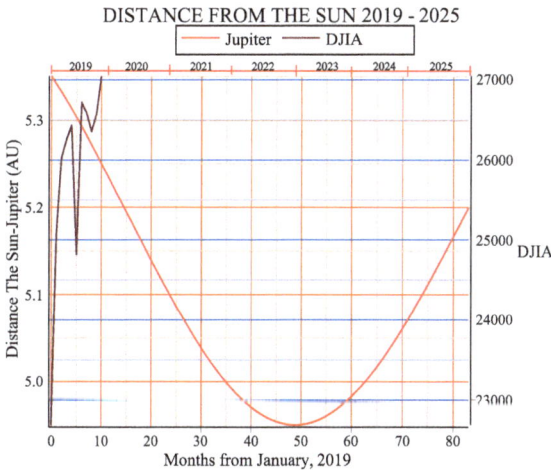

Figure 4.3: Distance the Sun-Jupiter with time

Figure 4.3 shows the distance of Jupiter from the Sun in Astronomical Units (AU) for the period 2019-2025. Jupiter reached its maximum distance from the Sun early in 2017, after which it began to get closer to it. In the past we found that the further Jupiter is from the Sun the more positive its influence on the market. Conversely, as this distance decreases, it may have a negative effect on the market. This distance will be close to its minimum value by the end of 2022, and will begin to increase after that.

Now, let us examine the distance of Saturn from the Sun (Figure 4.4). The same observations about the effect of the distance of Jupiter to the Sun apply to that of Saturn to the Sun. Saturn's distance to the Sun has been increasing during the current bull market, perhaps aiding the effect of an increasing MGP. It reached its farthest point from the Sun during the first months of 2018, after which it began to get closer to the Sun.

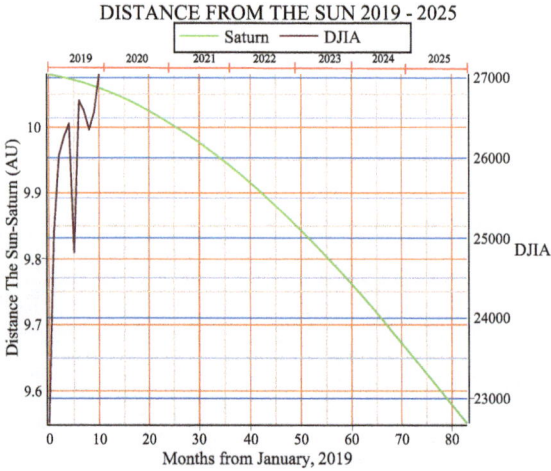

Figure 4.4: Distance the Sun-Saturn with time

Thus, the period 2020-2022 will experience a declining distance of Jupiter to the Sun, a declining distance of Saturn to the Sun, and a declining MGP. After 2022, the distance the Sun-Jupiter will begin to increase again, but the distance the Sun-Saturn and the MGP will continue to decline. In addition, there will be a Jupiter equinox in May 2021, and a Saturn equinox in May 2025 which may further cause a rapid decline in the market. The MGP descending cycle after 2020 may not in fact manifest immediately. From historical records, we saw that sometimes a descending trend in the MGP manifests quickly after it begins. For example, see Figures 3.7 and 3.9 (Chapter 3) for the bear market of 2000-2003. Other times, a descending MGP affects the market towards the end of its cycle. See for example Figure 3.4 for the Great Recession of 2007-2009.

For consistency with the analysis of Chapter 3, I include a graph of the future time evolution of the distance from the Earth to Jupiter (Figure 4.5), and one of the distance from the Earth to Saturn (Figure 4.6). I found that sometimes as the distance of these planets to the Earth increases, they may have a positive effect on the market, whereas when as distance decreases they may have a negative effect on the market. However, we found that these effects may have been secondary or perhaps temporary, and they did not always manifest consistently in all of the historical events studied. For this reason, I only include them here for observation purposes. Future research may confirm or disprove the influence of the distance of planets to the Earth.

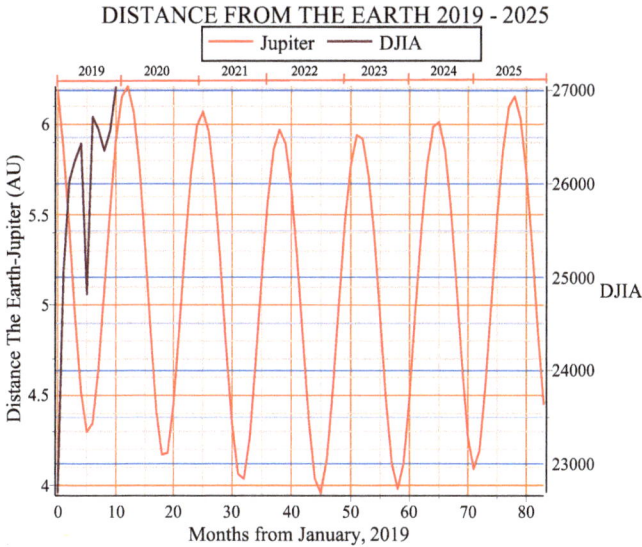

Figure 4.5: Distance the Earth-Jupiter with time

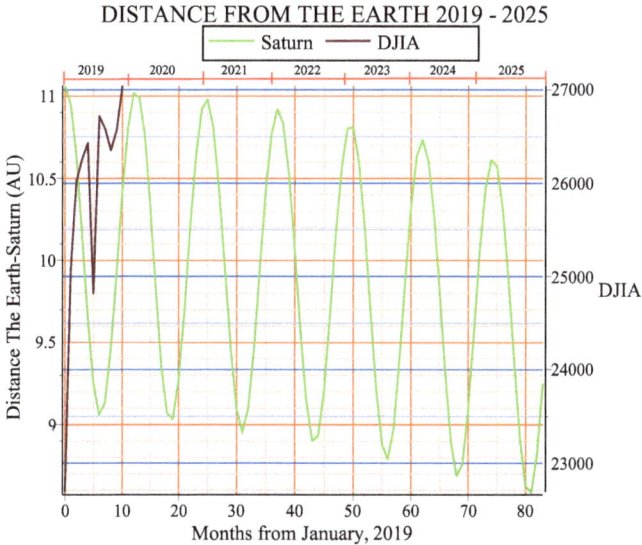

Figure 4.6: Distance the Earth-Saturn with time

From the information above, it appears that the astronomical environment is propitious for a few more months of the current bull market, after which the potential conditions for a declining cycle will follow. Wether or not the potential astronomical conditions will reflect in actual market moves remain to be seen. Considering other aspects, as of this writing the economy in the U. S. continues to grow at a robust pace, the unemployment rate is at a minimum, and investors confidence is at an all time high. The political climate, however, shows signs of instability with the potential for new conflicts in and out of the country. On the other hand, some investors warn that a market correction is imminent; some even suggest that the next drop in the DJIA will be of the order of 4,000 points.

Are you prepared, psychologically and financially, for the upcoming drop? It certainly helps to know that the astronomical potential for a market decline is imminent. Take the reins of your financial future; use the Cosmic Cycles to plan and act. I will share with you my strategy: Recently, I rebalanced my portfolios in all of my pretax (IRA's) and after-tax accounts. After several years of a bull market, the stocks portion was exceedingly high in valuation. I sold a portion of the equity at a high price and made a good profit. I invested some of the profits in bonds, which are very inexpensive now. A portion of the profits are sitting in a money market fund waiting to be used for a strategic purchase of stocks when the market declines significantly. These are companies with great financials in industries I like. I research them frequently, and in the past I have bought and sold their shares at the right time. Right now, stocks in these companies are unbelievably expensive. I shall wait until their shares drop in value. The only thing to do now is to wait, patiently, until the astronomical environment manifests in the market.

There is another portion of the profits that I will be using to pay for our next trip to Europe. As in the past, my wife and I plan to fly to Madrid, take the high-speed train to a small medieval village we like, not far from Valencia. We will rent a house, and spend a few weeks enjoying the historic sights. I see myself going every day to the market, leisurely talking with the locals, buying exotic ingredients, including local wine in bulk. I shall prepare my favorite paella with "the works" (e.g., chorizo, pork, garbanzo beans, sweet peppers, onions, garlic, and generous portions of olive oil).

We will then rent a car and travel across the Pyrenees into France. There is a lovely village, not far from Toulouse, where we plan to stay for a few weeks. We will rent a remodeled 19th century house. I can see myself enjoying the pastoral evenings in the back patio, slowly sipping a cognac, listening to the wind caressing the olive trees and the vineyards, and the languid sound of water dripping at an old fountain. I shall try to spot Jupiter in the magnificent Mediterranean sky, which will be pretty close to Saturn at this time. I will salute them and thank the Universal Intelligence for revealing the secrets of the Cosmic Cycles, and for giving me the clarity to use them.

I sincerely hope, with all my heart, that you will accomplish all of your goals, whatever they are –tangible or intangible–, while successfully *Riding the Waves of the Stock Market*. If the principles proposed in these lines help you attain your objectives, this book will have found its purpose. May life be good to you and your loved ones.

APPENDIX A: THE MATHEMATICS OF
ASTRONOMICAL POSITIONS

For completion, in this appendix I include a brief description about the mathematical formulae I used in the calculation of astronomical positions, angular distances between the various planets, distances from the planets to the Sun, and distances to the Earth. This is intended to those readers interested in the inside equations of the mathematical model I used in the present research. We described the methodology in Chapter 2, which culminated with the design of a master computer program in MAPLE. This appendix is also intended to those readers with a mathematical or engineering background who are interested in continuing the research in this fascinating field. Here we assume a familiarity with celestial mechanics, astronomy, and spherical trigonometry, since no theoretical explanations are included. For the theory and detailed descriptions of the equations below, the reader is referred to standard textbooks on the topic (e.g., Smart, 1986). Also, no explanations on the construction of the numerical algorithm or programming of the equations are given. These are treated at length in standard texts (e.g., Meeus, 1991; Duffet-Smith, 1988).

Calculating the Coordinates of a Planet

In this section, we follow the steps outlined in Duffet-Smith (1988). The first step is to calculate the position of the planet in its own orbital plane. Then, we project the planet's calculated position onto the plane of the ecliptic and find the ecliptic longitude and latitude referred to the Sun. These are called the *heliocentric* coordinates. Then, we transform from the Sun to the Earth to find the ecliptic coordinates referred to the Earth.

The first thing is to define an epoch upon which we base our calculations, a time where planetary orbits were precisely known. We chose January 0.0, 1990. Table A.1 shows the planetary orbits for this time. Next, we calculate the number of days, D, from the epoch to the desired date. Here we need to take into account the number of days to the beginning of the year since the epoch plus the number of days in the year to the date of calculation –usually the first business day of a month. The number of days in leap years must be included. Also, if the calculation date is earlier than the epoch, then D is negative.

Next, we find the *mean anomaly*, M, which refers to the motion of a fictitious planet, P_1, moving in a circle –instead of an ellipse– at constant speed with the same orbital period as that of the real planet. The mean anomaly is given by

$$M = \frac{360}{365.242191} \times \frac{D}{T_P} + \varepsilon - \bar{\omega},$$

(A.1)

where
   M=mean anomaly in degrees,
   T_p =orbital period of the planet in tropical years (Table A.1),
   ε =mean longitude of the planet at the epoch in degrees (Table A.1),
   $\bar{\omega}$ =longitude of the perihelion in degrees (Table A.1).

Table A.1: Elements of planetary orbits, Epoch January 0.0, 1990

Planet	T_p (years)	ε (degrees)	$\bar{\omega}$ (degrees)	e	a (AU)	i (degrees)	Ω (degrees)
Earth	1.00004	99.403308	102.768413	0.016713	1.000000	–	–
Jupiter	11.863075	90.638185	14.170747	0.048482	5.202561	1.303613	100.353142
Saturn	29.471362	287.690033	92.861407	0.055581	9.554747	2.488980	113.576139
Uranus	84.039492	271.063148	172.884833	0.046321	19.21814	0.773059	73.926961

Source: Duffet-Smith, 1988

Next, we calculate the *true anomaly*, v, which is the angle the real planet actually makes with the line between the Sun and the perihelion:

$$v=M+\frac{360}{\pi}e\sin(M),\qquad\text{(A.2)}$$

where
   v=the true anomaly in degrees,
   e=eccentricity of the planet's orbit (Table A.1),
   π=3.1415927   .

Next, we calculate the heliocentric longitude, l, given by

$$l=v+\bar{\omega},\qquad\text{(A.3)}$$

where
   l=heliocentric longitude in degrees.

Substituting Eq.(A.1) and Eq. (A.2) into Eq. (A.3), we obtain

$$l=\left(\frac{360}{365.242191}\times\frac{D}{T_P}\right)+\frac{360}{\pi}e\sin\left(\frac{360}{365.242191}\times\frac{D}{T_P}+\varepsilon-\bar{\omega}\right)+\varepsilon\qquad\text{(A.4)}$$

The line joining the principal focus of the planet's orbital ellipse (i.e., the Sun) and the planet's position is called the *radius vector*, r. It is given by

$$r=\frac{a(1-e^2)}{1+e\cos(v)},\qquad\text{(A.5)}$$

where
$r=$ the radius vector in AU, or the distance from the Sun to the planet,
$a=$the semi-major axis of the planet's orbit in AU (Table A.1), or half of the longest diameter of the planet's orbital ellipse.

The above calculations for the planet must be repeated for the Earth as well. Thus, we denote the values derived for the planet with lower case letters and those derived for the Earth with capital letters. Hence, we calculate l and r for the planet and L and R for the Earth, respectively.

Now, we calculate the heliocentric latitude of the planet as

$$\psi=\sin^{-1}(\sin(l-\Omega)\sin(i)), \qquad (A.6)$$

where
ψ =heliocentric latitude of the planet in degrees,
$i=$inclination of the planet's orbit in degrees (Table A.1),
Ω =longitude of the *ascending node* in degrees (Table A.1).

As the planet moves in its elliptical orbit, it is inclined an angle i with respect to the plane of the ecliptic. The *ascending node* of a planet is the point where it rises above the plane of the ecliptic, and the *descending node* of a planet is the point where it descends below the plane of the ecliptic. Since for the Earth $i=0$, then the heliocentric latitude of the Earth is zero.

Now, project the calculations for the planet onto the plane of the ecliptic to find the projected heliocentric longitude, l', and the projected radius vector, r':

$$l'=\tan^{-1}(\tan(l-\Omega)\cos(i))+\Omega$$
$$r'=r\cos(\psi). \qquad (A.7)$$

where
$l'=$the planet's heliocentric longitude projected onto the plane of the ecliptic in degrees,
$r'=$the planet's heliocentric radius vector projected onto the plane of the ecliptic in degrees.

The next step is to refer the above calculations to the Earth in order to find the geocentric ecliptic latitude, β, and the longitude, λ, of the planet. For the outer planets –Mars, Jupiter, Uranus, or Neptune–, the longitude is given by

$$\lambda=\tan^{-1}\left(\frac{R\sin(l'-L)}{r'-R\cos(l'-L)}\right), \qquad (A.8)$$

where
$\lambda=$geocentric ecliptic longitude for the planet in degrees.

For the inner planets –Mercury, and Venus–, the longitude is given by

$$\lambda=180+L+\tan^{-1}\left(\frac{r'\sin(L-l')}{R-r'\cos(L-l')}\right). \qquad (A.9)$$

To calculate the latitude for either an inner or an outer planet, we use the following formula:

$$\beta = \tan^{-1}\left(\frac{r'\tan(\psi)\sin(\lambda - l')}{R\sin(l' - L)}\right),$$

(A.10)

where
β = geocentric ecliptic latitude for the planet in degrees.

Computational Procedure
The procedure for the calculation of the astronomical position of a planet on a desired date is summarized as follows:

1. Calculate the number of says, D, since the epoch, January 0.0, 1990.

Calculations for the planet (subscript P denotes "for the planet").

2. From Eq. (A.1), calculate

$$N_P = \frac{360}{365.242191} \times \frac{D}{T_P}.$$

(A.11)

Subtract multiples of 360 to bring the result into the range 0-360 degrees.

3. From Eqs. (A.1) and (A.11), calculate

$$M_P = N_P + \varepsilon - \bar{\omega}.$$

(A.12)

4. From Eqs. (A.4), (A.11), and (A.12), calculate

$$l = N_P + \frac{360}{\pi}e\sin(M_P) + \varepsilon.$$

(A.13)

If the result is greater than 360 degrees, subtract 360. If the result is negative, add 360.

5. From Eqs. (A.3) and (A.13),

$$v_P = l - \bar{\omega}.$$

(A.14)

6. From Eqs. (A.5) and (A.14), calculate the radius vector.

$$r = \frac{a(1 - e^2)}{1 + e\cos(v_P)}.$$

(A.15)

Calculations for the Earth (subscript E denotes "for the Earth").

7. From Eq. (A.1),

$$N_E = \frac{360}{365.242191} \times \frac{D}{T_E}.$$

(A.16)

Subtract multiples of 360 to bring the result within the range of 0-360.

8. From Eqs. (A.1) and (A.16), calculate

$$M_E = N_E + \varepsilon - \bar{\omega}.$$ (A.17)

9. From Eqs. (A.4), (A.16), and (A.17), calculate

$$L = N_E + \frac{360}{\pi} e \sin(M_E) + \varepsilon.$$ (A.18)

If the result is greater than 360 degrees, subtract 360. If the result is negative, add 360.

10. From Eqs. (A.3) and (A.18),

$$v_E = L - \bar{\omega}.$$ (A.19)

11. From Eqs. (A.5) and (A.19),

$$R = \frac{a(1 - e^2)}{1 + e\cos(v_E)}.$$ (A.20)

12. From Eq. (A.6), calculate the heliocentric latitude of the planet:

$$\psi = \sin^{-1}(\sin(l - \Omega)\sin(i)),$$ (A.21)

In the next three steps, we implement Eq.(A.7) to find the projected heliocentric longitude of the planet.

13. From the top Eq. (A.7), calculate the following, while remembering the identity $\tan(\theta) = \sin(\theta)/\cos(\theta)$:

$$y = \sin(l - \Omega)\cos(i).$$ (A.22)

14. Calculate

$$x = \cos(l - \Omega).$$ (A.23)

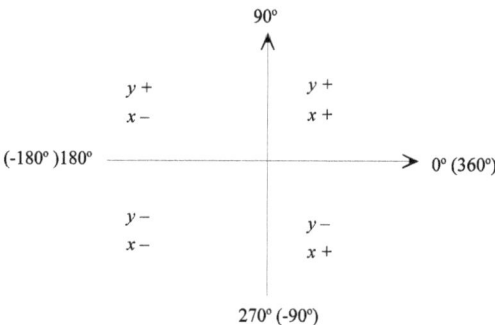

Figure A.1: Removing the ambiguity when taking $\tan^{-1}(y/x)$

15. Calculate

$$\theta = \tan^{-1}\left(\frac{y}{x}\right). \tag{A.24}$$

We have to remove the ambiguity which arises when taking the inverse tangent. The rule dictates that θ should be in the quadrant indicated by the signs of y and x (Figure A.1). Thus, add or subtract 180 or 360 to θ to bring it into the correct quadrant, unless it is already there.

16. From Eqs. (A.7) and (A.24),

$$l' = \theta + \Omega. \tag{A.25}$$

Verify that l' should close in value to l.

17. From the bottom Eq. (A7) and Eq. (A.21),

$$r' = r\cos(\psi). \tag{A.26}$$

18. Calculate the geocentric longitude of the planet. For an outer planet, use Eq. (A.8) (along with Eqs. (A.18), (A.20), (A.25), and (2.26)):

$$\lambda = \tan^{-1}\left(\frac{R\sin(l'-L)}{r'-R\cos(l'-L)}\right), \tag{A.27}$$

If the answer is negative, add 360. If the answer is more than 360, subtract 360.

For an inner planet, use Eq. (A.9) (along with Eqs. (A.18), (A.20), (A.25), and (2.26)). First calculate

$$\lambda = 180 + L + \tan^{-1}\left(\frac{r'\sin(L-l')}{R-r'\cos(L-l')}\right). \tag{A.28}$$

Again, if the answer is negative, add 360. If the answer is more than 360, subtract 360.

19. Finally, from Eq. (A.10), (A.18), (A.20), (A.25), (2.26), and (A.28), find the geocentric longitude:

$$\beta = \tan^{-1}\left(\frac{r'\tan(\psi)\sin(\lambda-l')}{R\sin(l'-L)}\right), \tag{A.29}$$

Steps 1 through 19 are needed to calculate the astronomical position of a planet at a fixed date. In our simulations, we calculated the position of the planets on the first business day of each month from 1900 to 2025. This means that the above steps must be repeated for each planet and for each date required in the simulations. This is part of the mathematical model whose structure is described in the 10 steps outlined in Chapter 2.

All of the equations described in this appendix were programmed in MAPLE and used to generate the graphics shown in Chapters 2, 3, and 4.

Calculating Angular Distances and Linear Distances

To calculate the distance from a planet to the Sun, r, at a given date, we use Eq. (A.15). To calculate the distance from the Earth to the Sun, R, we use Eq. (A.20). Also, we can use the formulae in the last section to calculate the distance from the Earth to any planet:

$$\rho=\sqrt{R^2+r^2-2Rr\cos(l-L)}, \tag{A.30}$$

where
  ρ=distance form the Earth to a planet in AU, and the rest of the terms
    as defined before.

Now, to calculate the angular distance between two planets in the sky, we need their ecliptic coordinates and the following formula:

$$d=\sqrt{\cos^2\left(\frac{\beta_1+\beta_2}{2}\right)\cdot\Delta\lambda^2+\Delta\beta^2,} \tag{A.31}$$

where
  d=angle between two planets in degrees,
  $\Delta\lambda=\lambda_1-\lambda_2$, longitude difference between the to planets in degrees,
  λ_1 =ecliptic longitude of planet 1 in degrees,
  λ_2 =ecliptic longitude of planet 2 in degrees,
  $\Delta\beta=\beta_1-\beta_2$ =latitude difference between the two planets in degrees,
  β_1 =ecliptic latitude of planet 1 in degrees,
  β_2 =ecliptic latitude of planet 2 in degrees.

Once again, these calculations were conducted for the first business day of each month from 1900 to 2025, and used to obtain the graphs shown in Chapters 3 and 4.

"Sometimes, it is necessary that a poet becomes wealthy: He would show the rich what one can do with money."

Abel Bonnard (1883 - 1968).

"The best limitation of money is that which prevents us from falling into poverty, or stray too far from it."

Luccio Anneo Séneca (4 BC - 65 CE).

BIBLIOGRAPHY

America's Best History, 1900-2017. Illustrated History of the United States. http://americasbesthistory.com

Belsky, Gary and Gilovich, Thomas, 1999. *Why Smart People Make Big Mistakes – and How to Correct Them. Lessons from the New Science of Behavioral Economics.* Simon & Schuster, New York, NY.

Benner, Samuel, 1884. *Benner's Prophecies of Future Ups and Downs in Prices: What Years to Make Money on Pig-iron, Hogs, Corn, and Provisions.* Third ed. Robert Clarke & Co., Cincinnati, OH.

Bernstein, William, 2002. *The Four pillars of Investing: Lessons for Building a Winning Portfolio.* McGraw-Hill, New York, NY.

Bradley, Donald A., 1984. *Stock Market Prediction.* 2nd Ed. Llewellyn Publications, St. Paul, MN.

Clason, George S., 2002. *The Richest Man in Babylon.* New American Library (Penguin), New York, NY.

Dewey, Edward R., and Dakin, Edwin F., 2010. *Cycles: The Science of Prediction.* Foundation for the Study of Cycles. Henry Holt & Co. Reprinted by Kessinger Legacy Reprints. Whitefish, MN, 2010.

Duffet-Smith, Peter, 1988. *Practical Astronomy with Your Calculator.* 3rd Ed. Cambridge University Press, Cambridge, U. K.

Ellis, Charles, 2002. *Winning the Loser's Game: Timeless Strategies for Successful Investment.* McGraw-Hill, New York, NY.

Emery, , 1995. *Watergate: The Corruption of American Politics and the Fall of Richard Nixon.* Touchstone, New York, NY.

Farrell, Paul., 2006. *The Lazy Person's Guide to Investing: A book for Procrastinators, the Financially Challenged, and Everyone Who Worries About Dealing with Their Money.* Warner Books, New York, NY.

Hirsch, Jeffrey A., 2012. *The Little Book of Stock Market Cycles: How to Take Advantage of Time-Proven Market Patters.* Wiley. New York, NY.

Justice, Paul, 2009. *Warning: Leveraged and Inverse ETFs Kill Portfolios.* Morningstar, Inc., http://news.morningstar.com/articlenet/article.aspx?id=271892

Lewis, H. Spencer, 1994. *Self Mastery and Fate with the Cycles of Life.* The Rosicrucian order, AMORC. San jose, CA.

Lewis, H. S., 1981. Mansions of the Soul. Supreme Grand Lodge of AMORC, Inc., San Jose, CA.

Lynch, Peter., and Rothchild, John, 1989. *One Up On Wall Street. How to Use What You Already Know to Make Money in the Market.* Penguin Books, New York, NY.

Macrotrends, LLC., 2017. *Dow Jones - 100 Year Historical Chart.* Http://www.macrotrends.com

Merriman, Paul, 2008. *Live It Up Without Outliving Your Money. Getting The Most From Your Investments in Retirement.* John Wiley & Sons, Hoboken, NJ.

Meeus, Jean, 1991. *Astronomical Algorithms.* Willmann-Bell Inc., Richmond, VA.

National Aeronautics and Space Administration (NASA). *Solar System Dynamics: Horizons System.* California Institute of Technology, Jet Propulsion Laboratory, https://ssd.jpl.nasa.gov/horizons.cgi

Salomon, S., 2011. *It is in your Hands: Emotional Freedom Technique (EFT): The Power to Eliminate Stress, Anxiety, and All Negative Emotions.* 2nd Ed. SpiralPress, Ambler, PA

Schultheis, Bill., 2013. *The Coffeehouse Investor: How to Build Wealth, Ignore Wall Street, and Get On with Your Life* . Penguin, New York, NY.

Serrano, S. E., 2011. *The Three Spirits: Applications of Huna to Health, Prosperity, and Personal Growth.* Second Ed. SpiralPress, Ambler, PA.

Smart, W. M., 1986. *Textbook on Spherical Astronomy.* 6th Ed. Rev. by R. M. Green. Cambridge University Press. Cambridge, U. K.

Swedroe, Larry, 2003. *The Successful Investor Today.* Truman Talley Books, New York, NY.

Taleb, Nassim, 2005. *Fooled by Randomness. The Hidden Role of Chance in Life and in the Markets.* Random House, New York, NY.

Tice, John, H., 1875. *Elements of Meteorology, Part II: Meteorological Cycles.* Meteorological Research and Publication Company. Saint Louis, MO.

Wikipedia, 2017. *The Free Encyclopedia.* https://www.wikipedia.org

Zweig, Jason, 2007. *Your Money and Your Brain. How the New Science of Neuroeconomics Can Help Make You Rich.* Simon & Schuster, New York, NY.

INDEX

AN ART OF LIVING

André Maurois

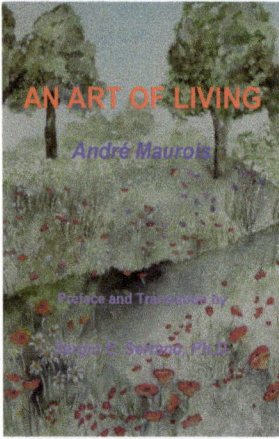

A new translation by Sergio E. Serrano of this inspirational book containing sound advice on the art of living by the French historian, biographer, and philosopher, André Maurois (1885-1967), who was one of the most celebrated and prolific writers of the 20th century.

- **Timeless wisdom and advice on the art of living for today's young and old**
- **The art of thinking**
- **The art of loving**
- **The art of working**
- **The art of leadership**
- **The art of growing old**

Maurois speaks to the soul of the reader. The principles he conveys remain as valid and as useful in the 21st century as they were in the 20th

According to Maurois, our lives are works of art, expressions of inner beauty, conceived and created by our inner selves, tested by the circumstances and experiences of life, perfected and modified by the learning and growth resulting from these experiences.

Maurois speaks to the soul of the reader. The principles he conveys remain as valid and as useful in the 21st century as they were in the 20th.

Maurois accurately predicted:

- **The ultimate failure of all social revolutions**
- **The necessity of slow change in human customs and attitudes as a key to lasting changes**
- **The technological development and implementation of robots in large assembly lines**
- **The characteristics of a reasonable and effective government**
- **The inner virtues to cultivate in order to successfully overcome the adversities of life**
- **The qualities to seek in order to maintain stable, loving, relationships**
- **The attributes to encourage as an effective manager**
- **The essentials by which to plan a long and enjoyable retirement**
- **The principles behind an effective educational system**

An Art of Living remained out of print for several decades. This new translation resurrects this little treasure of a book for the English readers of today; it remains faithful to the original French edition and to the style of the author.

THE THREE SPIRITS

Applications of Huna to Health, Prosperity, and personal Growth

Sergio E, Serrano, Ph.D.

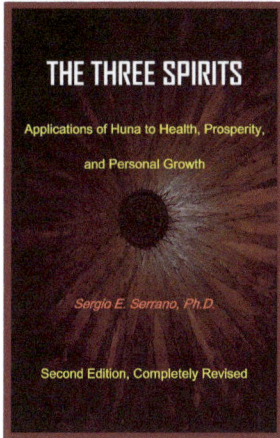

"If you are not using Huna, you are working too hard."

Max Freedom Long, author of "The secret Science Behind Miracles."

A modern application of ancient Hawaiian mysticism (i.e., Huna) with many practical exercises to understand the structure of our inner mind, discover extraordinary latent abilities, improve health, increase wealth, achieve professional objectives, enrich relationships with others, eliminate stress and anxiety, and enhance spiritual development.

- Huna means "secret" in the Hawaiian language. It refers to the coded knowledge of the ancient Kahunas, who were known for healing the sick, controlling the weather, walking over hot lava, and predicting and changing the future

- Know the forces and meet the entities of the mind that control the art of mental creation

- Includes many step-by-step practical exercises to develop and use the skills necessary to effectively and efficiently achieve personal or professional desires

- Huna techniques are combined with Emotional Freedom Technique (EFT), which are energy therapies similar to acupuncture

- Includes many step-by-step practical exercises to effectively remove psychological fixations, complexes, fears, anxiety, phobias, and negative emotions, without the need of expensive "talk therapies"

- Written in a simple style, with many practical exercises and illustrations to gradually develop and apply the principles

- Anyone who takes the time to apply Huna can soon achieve important results to improve his/her life

IT IS IN YOUR HANDS:
EMOTIONAL FREEDOM TECHNIQUE (EFT)

The Power to Eliminate Stress, Anxiety,
and All Negative Emotions

Sobeida Salomon, Ph.D.

An introduction to a new psychological therapeutic method called Emotional Freedom Technique (EFT). It is a practical procedure to eliminate all negative emotions, including stress, anxiety, fears, phobias, past traumas (including Post Traumatic Stress Disorder, PTSD), substance abuse, and all addictions.

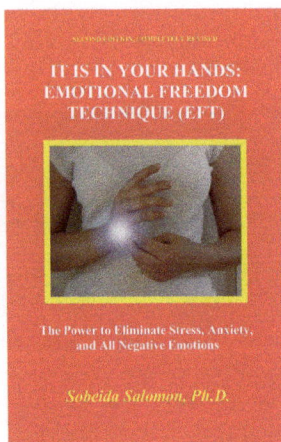

- **With EFT the user no longer has to go through months of expensive, and usually ineffective, conventional "talk therapies."**

- **Anyone can be free from any negative emotional or psychological difficulty that in the past has prevented him/her from reaching full potential, or from living a joyful, blissful life.**

- **EFT puts in your hands the power to eliminate all negative emotions. It is simple, effective, and most importantly, it is free!**

Emotional Freedom Technique (EFT) and Thought Field Therapies (TFT) access the body's energy meridian system to release the negative energy attached to a particular negative emotion. The energy meridian system is a natural network of energy pathways circulating throughout the body. EFT uses the same principles of energy therapies, such as acupuncture, except that EFT does not require needles and it heals psychological problems, not just physical ones.

EFT/TFT is the outcome of a recent scientific discovery that found that the cause of negative emotions is not the memory of a traumatic event, but the negative energy entangled around the memory. This finding shows that by releasing this energy, the negative emotion is instantly eliminated. Thousands of people have reported relief from past traumas and negative feelings that had previously defied months of conventional treatment.

The reader only needs to learn a series of meridian end points, how to use the hands to tap on these points for a few minutes, and the ability to concentrate and feel a particular negative emotion. It is that simple! IT IS IN YOUR HANDS is written in a simple style, with many practical exercises, case studies to treat specific negative emotions, and illustrations designed to gradually develop and apply the principles.

ENGINEERING UNCERTAINTY AND RISK ANALYSIS

A Balanced Approach to Probability, Statistics, Stochastic Modeling, and Stochastic Differential Equations

Sergio E. Serrano, Ph.D.

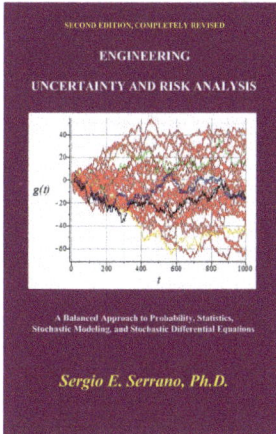

An integrated coverage of probability, statistics, Monte Carlo simulation, inferential statistics, design of experiments, systems reliability, fitting random data to models, analysis of variance, stochastic processes, and stochastic differential equations for engineers and scientists. The author for the first time presents an introduction to the broad field of applied engineering uncertainty analysis in one comprehensive, friendly, coverage.

- Each concept is illustrated with several examples of relevance in engineering applications (no cards, colored balls, or dice)

- 478 pages; 177 solved examples; 147 proposed problems; 174 illustrations, 69 short computer programs; and 51 data and statistical tables

- Clear presentation of concepts. Practical engineering examples. No cards, no dice, no colored balls

- Prepares the reader for today's problems in engineering analysis, modeling, and design under uncertainty

- This edition includes new research advances in nonlinear stochastic differential equations; simple methods to solve and graph boundary-value problems in several dimensions

- Integrated treatment of probability, statistics, and stochastic modeling

- Includes numerical (Monte Carlo) simulations and analytical modeling

- Intuitive and graphical introduction to stochastic processes. Practical introduction to applied stochastic differential equations